D1299281

MAR 2 5 2016

1st EDITION

Perspectives on Modern World History

Hurricane Katrina

1st EDITION

Perspectives on Modern World History

Hurricane Katrina

Ebonie Ledbetter

Editor

GREENHAVEN PRESS
A part of Gale, Cengage Learning

GALE
CENGAGE Learning

Farmington Hills, Mich • San Francisco • New York • Waterville, Maine
Meriden. Conn • Mason. Ohio • Chicago

Patricia Coryell, *Vice President @ Publisher, New Products and GVRL*
Douglas Dentino, *Manager, New Product*
Judy Galens, *Acquisitions Editor*

© 2015 Greenhaven Press, a part of Gale, Cengage Learning.

WCN: 01-100-101

Articles in Greenhaven Press anthologies are often edited for length to meet page requirements. In addition, original titles of these works are changed to clearly present the main thesis and to explicitly indicate the author's opinion. Every effort is made to ensure that Greenhaven Press accurately reflects the original intent of the authors. Every effort has been made to trace the owners of copyrighted material.

Cover images © Tand Denson/Shutterstock.com and © FEMA/Alamy.

LIBRARY OF CONGRESS CATALOGING-IN-PUBLICATION DATA

Hurricane Katrina / Ebonie Ledbetter, book editor.
    pages cm. -- (Perspectives on modern world history)
 Includes bibliographical references and index.
 ISBN 978-0-7377-7309-5 (hardcover)
1. Hurricane Katrina, 2005. 2. Disasters--Louisiana--New Orleans--History--21st century. 3. New Orleans (La.)--History--21st century. I. Ledbetter, Ebonie.
 HV636 2005 .N4 H86 2015
 976'.044--dc23

                                                                                    2014041991

Printed in the United States of America
1 2 3 4 5 6 7 19 18 17 16 15

CONTENTS

CHAPTER 1   ## Historical Background on Hurricane Katrina

1. A Category-Three Hurricane Wreaks Havoc on the Gulf Coast

American Decades: 2000–2009

In August 2005, Hurricane Katrina devastated the Gulf Coast region of the United States. The editors of a historical encyclopedia summarize the events that occurred before, during, and after the storm.

2. Old West Has Nothing on Katrina Aftermath

Brian Thevenot, Keith Spera, and Doug MacCash

Journalists in New Orleans report on the aftermath of Hurricane Katrina as floodwaters continue to rise and residents become stranded in the area.

3. The US Government Responds to Hurricane Katrina

Michael Chertoff

In a news briefing, the secretary of the US Department of Homeland Security describes the measures the government is taking to deal

with the crisis and notes that it is the largest
relief effort in US history.

CHAPTER 2 Controversies Surrounding Hurricane
Katrina

explains why he was faulted for the government's ineffective response to the storm.

FOREWORD

"History cannot give us a program for the future, but it can give us a fuller understanding of ourselves, and of our common humanity, so that we can better face the future."

—Robert Penn Warren,
American poet and novelist

The history of each nation is punctuated by momentous events that represent turning points for that nation, with an impact felt far beyond its borders. These events—displaying the full range of human capabilities, from violence, greed, and ignorance to heroism, courage, and strength—are nearly always complicated and multifaceted. Any student of history faces the challenge of grasping the many strands that constitute such world-changing events as wars, social movements, and environmental disasters. But understanding these significant historic events can be enhanced by exposure to a variety of perspectives, whether of people involved intimately or of ones observing from a distance of miles or years. Understanding can also be increased by learning about the controversies surrounding such events and exploring hot-button issues from multiple angles. Finally, true understanding of important historic events involves knowledge of the events' human impact—of the ways such events affected people in their everyday lives—all over the world.

Perspectives on Modern World History examines global historic events from the twentieth century onward by presenting analysis and observation from numerous vantage points. Each volume offers high school, early college level, and general interest readers a thematically arranged anthology of previously published materials that address a major historical event, with an emphasis on international coverage. Each volume opens with background information on the event, then presents the controversies surrounding that event, and concludes with first-person narratives from people who lived through the event or were affected by it. By providing primary sources from the time of the event, as well as relevant commentary surrounding the event, this series can be used to inform debate, help develop critical thinking skills, increase global awareness, and enhance an understanding of international perspectives on history.

Material in each volume is selected from a diverse range of sources, including journals, magazines, newspapers, nonfiction books, personal narratives, speeches, congressional testimony, government documents, pamphlets, organization newsletters, and position papers. Articles taken from these sources are carefully edited and introduced to provide context and background. Each volume of Perspectives on Modern World History includes an array of views on events of global significance. Much of the material comes from international sources and from US sources that provide extensive international coverage.

Each volume in the Perspectives on Modern World History series also includes:

- A full-color **world map**, offering context and geographic perspective.
- An annotated **table of contents** that provides a brief summary of each essay in the volume.
- An **introduction** specific to the volume topic.
- For each viewpoint, a brief **introduction** that has notes about the author and source of the viewpoint, and that provides a summary of its main points.
- Full-color **charts, graphs, maps**, and other visual representations.

- Informational **sidebars** that explore the lives of key individuals, give background on historical events, or explain scientific or technical concepts.
- A **glossary** that defines key terms, as needed.
- A **chronology** of important dates preceding, during, and immediately following the event.
- A **bibliography** of additional books, periodicals, and websites for further research.
- A comprehensive **subject index** that offers access to people, places, and events cited in the text.

Perspectives on Modern World History is designed for a broad spectrum of readers who want to learn more about not only history but also current events, political science, government, international relations, and sociology—students doing research for class assignments or debates, teachers and faculty seeking to supplement course materials, and others wanting to improve their understanding of history. Each volume of Perspectives on Modern World History is designed to illuminate a complicated event, to spark debate, and to show the human perspective behind the world's most significant happenings of recent decades.

INTRODUCTION

In August 2005, Hurricane Katrina made landfall in the Gulf Coast region of the United States as a category-three storm. While it is not the strongest or deadliest hurricane in US history, it holds the title of the costliest—causing more than $100 billion worth of damage. The storm was responsible for more than 1,300 deaths. A mismanaged response effort by the government compounded the destruction from the hurricane and transformed the storm into both a natural *and* man-made disaster.

Days before the storm reached the Gulf Coast, the National Hurricane Center (NHC) predicted it would be a "potentially catastrophic" hurricane, cause widespread damage, and potentially breach the levee system in New Orleans.[1] Governors throughout the region declared states of emergency and urged residents to evacuate. When the hurricane made landfall on August 29, it brought winds of up to 125 miles per hour. Katrina destroyed homes throughout the Gulf Coast and caused power and telecommunications outages. The storm also damaged oil rigs in the region, which led to a spike in gas prices.

In the midst of the calamity, the NHC prediction was proven true, and Katrina toppled the levees in New Orleans. Remaining residents were stranded as floodwaters entered the city. Chaos reigned as reports of lawlessness and looting spread throughout the area. Up to twenty thousand residents filled the Louisiana Superdome, which lacked power and sufficient resources for the evacuees. State and local officials begged the federal government for help evacuating residents from the city.

On September 1, New Orleans mayor Ray Nagin made a national plea on CNN. "This is a desperate SOS," he said. "Right now we are out of resources at the convention center and don't anticipate enough buses. We need buses. Currently the convention center is unsanitary and unsafe, and we're running out of supplies."[2] New Orleans residents remained trapped. Terry Ebbert, director of the New Orleans Office of Homeland Security, said:

> This is a national disgrace. FEMA [the Federal Emergency Management Agency] has been here three days, yet there is no command and control. . . . We can send massive amounts of aid [in 2004] to tsunami victims [in Japan], but we can't bail out the city of New Orleans. We have got a mayor who has been pushing and asking, but we're not getting supplies.[3]

The response of President George W. Bush only worsened the criticism of the federal government. The president was on vacation when the storm hit and did not depart his Crawford, Texas, ranch until August 31 to oversee the hurricane relief effort. He then gave a speech praising the actions of the government and the director of FEMA, Michael Brown, in particular.

Critics charged that the Bush administration was out of touch with the situation in the Gulf Coast.

President Bush admitted the government's initial actions were "unacceptable" and pledged that his administration would improve its efforts. On September 2 he said, "I want to assure the people of the affected areas and this country that we'll deploy the assets necessary to get the situation under control."[4] On the same day, Congress approved $10.5 billion in aid for rescue and relief. By September 3, a major airlift operation took place in New Orleans, and residents were evacuated from the city en masse.

Nations from around the world offered aid and technical assistance for the relief effort. However, they also lodged condemnation at the US government. In a September 4 article in the *Washington Post*, Kevin Sullivan wrote: "People around the world cannot believe what they're seeing. . . . How can this be happening, they ask, in a nation whose wealth and power seem almost supernatural in so many struggling corners of the world?"[5] In the midst of national and international criticism, Bush vowed to lead an investigation into how the government handled the catastrophe.

Congress approved nearly $140 billion in federal recovery funding for the Gulf Coast under President Bush. In the weeks, months, and years after the storm, the government oversaw cleanup efforts, the levees in New Orleans were rebuilt, and evacuees returned to the Gulf Coast. However, in the years after Katrina, the government's relief efforts came under criticism. By June 2006, it was reported that FEMA misappropriated nearly $2 billion in relief funds. "The blatant fraud, the audacity of the schemes, the scale of the waste—it is just breathtaking," said Republican senator Susan Collins.[6] In 2013 the Department of Housing and Urban Development found that millions of dollars in funds for home redevelopment were missing. David Montoya, inspector general of the agency, said:

> We have $700 million that we can't account for and that certainly did not go to elevating homes and preventing future damage from storms. . . . This is money that we don't get back and this is money that we can't put toward other disaster victims.[7]

In addition to the misappropriation of funds, investigations found that the US federal government failed to use more than $800 million in foreign aid. According to an article in the *Washington Post*, "officials turned down countless offers of allied troops and search-and-rescue teams," and "valuable supplies and services . . . were delayed or declined because the government could not handle them."[8]

In the aftermath of Katrina, numerous issues sparked controversy. Critics charged that officials failed to properly prepare for the storm and ignored the vulnerability of the New Orleans levee system. Others argued that the government's slow response stemmed from racism against the poor African Americans stranded in New Orleans. The media was accused of spreading misinformed reports of violence in New Orleans. Some argued that the nation disproportionately focused on New Orleans and ignored other areas throughout the region that were affected by the hurricane. The use of relief funds was also contested, and many government officials were charged with corruption.

Almost a decade later, the Gulf Coast is still recovering from Hurricane Katrina. The hurricane's legacy continues to stir debate, and the storm greatly affected public policy, the management of emergency response systems, and environmental protection regulation. *Perspectives in Modern World History: Hurricane Katrina* examines the events leading up to the hurricane, the immediate impact of the storm, and its lasting effect on US society.

Notes

1. National Hurricane Center, "Hurricane Katrina Advisory Number 24," August 28, 2005. www.nhc.noaa.gov.
2. Marc Sandalow, "Anarchy, Anger, Desperation/The Response/ Sharp Criticism of U.S. Reaction and Failure to Prevent Disaster," *SF Gate*, September 2, 2005. www.sfgate.com.
3. Josh White and Peter Whoriskey, "Planning, Response Are Faulted," *Washington Post*, September 2, 2005. www.washington post.com.
4. "Remarks on Departure for a Tour of Gulf Coast Areas Damaged by Hurricane Katrina," Public Papers of the Presidents of the United States: George W. Bush, 2005. www.gpo.gov.
5. Kevin Sullivan, "How Could This Be Happening in the United States?," *Washington Post*, September 4, 2005. www.washington post.com.
6. Eric Lipton, "'Breathtaking' Waste and Fraud in Hurricane Aid," *New York Times*, June 27, 2006. www.nytimes.com.
7. Jeff Zeleny, "$700 Million in Katrina Relief Missing, Report Shows," ABC News, April 3, 2013. http://abcnews.go.com.

8. John Solomon and Spencer S. Hsu, "Most Katrina Aid from Overseas Went Unclaimed," *Washington Post*, April 29, 2007. www .washingtonpost.com.

World Map

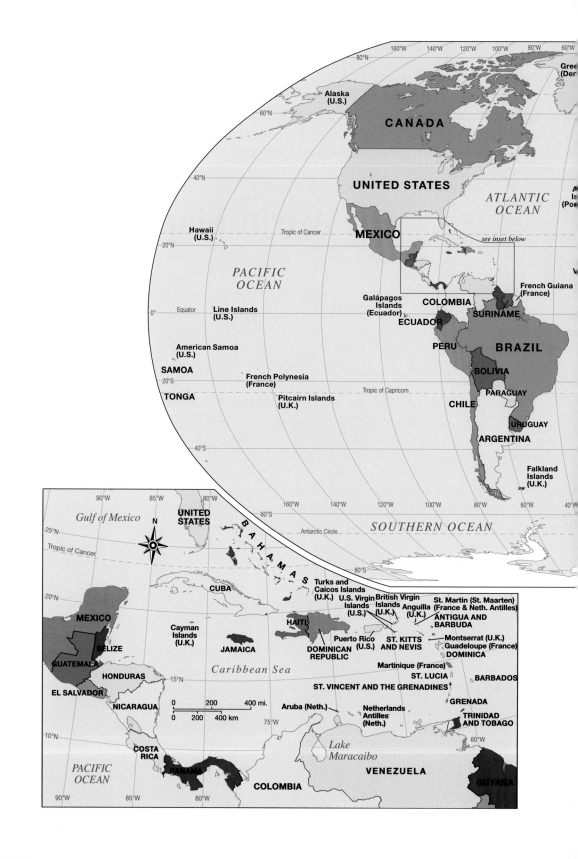

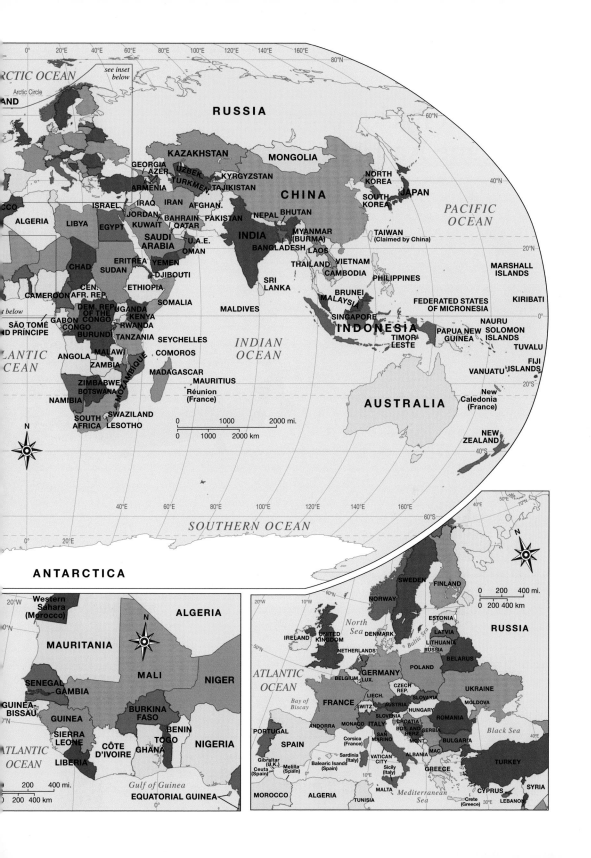

CHAPTER 1

Historical Background on Hurricane Katrina

A Category-Three Hurricane Wreaks Havoc on the Gulf Coast

American Decades: 2000–2009

The following viewpoint provides an overview of Hurricane Katrina, a storm that hit the Gulf Coast region of the United States in August 2005. The authors explain that the storm had a devastating impact on the region, taking lives and causing billions of dollars in property damage. They add that, in the aftermath of the storm, relief efforts were hindered by miscommunication as well as a lack of preparation. The US government's response to Katrina received nationwide criticism, state the authors, and the hurricane had a lasting impact on discussions about the effectiveness of federal and state emergency operations. *American Decades* is a historical encyclopedia covering the events, people, and social trends that have had an impact on contemporary history. The 2000–2009 edition was edited by historian Eric Bargeron and publishing manager James F. Tidd Jr., both based in Columbia, South Carolina.

Photo on opposite page: A military helicopter drops sandbags to plug a levee broken in the aftermath of Hurricane Katrina on September 11, 2005. (© Jerry Grayson/ Helifilms Australia PTY Ltd/Getty Images.)

SOURCE. Eric Bargeron and James F. Tidd Jr., eds, "Hurricane Katrina," *American Decades: 2000–2009*. Farmington Hills, MI: Gale, 2011, pp. 218–220. Copyright © 2011 Cengage Learning. All rights reserved. Reproduced with permission.

On Monday morning, 29 August 2005, Katrina, a category-three hurricane, slammed into America's Gulf Coast, wreaking havoc from Louisiana to Florida. Initial reports revealed a devastating storm that claimed more than one hundred lives and caused billions of dollars in property damage. The region's economy ground to a halt as cleanup efforts began. Highways were destroyed; homes were flooded; shuttered oil rigs raised gas prices; and coastal casinos were gutted. In New Orleans, for the first time since the Civil War, an entire city had been ordered to evacuate and abandon homes and businesses. New Orleans officials feared the worst in a city resting below sea level, protected by an aging system of levees. But after the storm passed by, many people of New Orleans—those who had fled, had stayed in their homes, or sought shelter—felt that they had escaped disaster. However, the following day, a major levee was breached, sending the muddy water from Lake Pontchartrain flooding into the city. Eighty percent of the city was submerged, leaving more than 100,000 people stranded.

> Millions . . . wondered how camera crews and news commentators had reached the city while federal and state relief organizations failed to bring assistance.

Citywide Disaster

In New Orleans, where many vulnerable citizens had attempted to weather the storm in homes or designated shelters such as the Superdome or convention center, more than 25,000 people spent six terrifying days in the Superdome. Most of them were old, sick, or simply too poor to leave the city. Days went by without electricity. The generators ran out of fuel, and the Superdome became sweltering, dark, and dangerous. Deaths and incidents of rape occurred while people waited to evacuate. Hospitals, too, lost power, and nurses and doctors attempted to keep patients alive with hand ventilators,

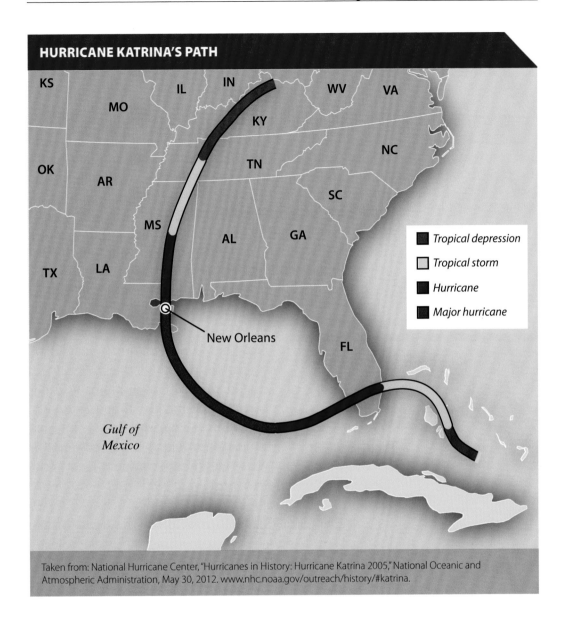

HURRICANE KATRINA'S PATH

Legend:
- Tropical depression
- Tropical storm
- Hurricane
- Major hurricane

New Orleans

Gulf of
Mexico

Taken from: National Hurricane Center, "Hurricanes in History: Hurricane Katrina 2005," National Oceanic and Atmospheric Administration, May 30, 2012. www.nhc.noaa.gov/outreach/history/#katrina.

food from vending machines, and dwindling supplies of bottled water. New Orleans's streets became rivers filled with sewage, chemicals, and debris. In some cases, people were forced to tear through their roofs hoping to be spotted by passing helicopters. Across the city, looters broke into stores and restaurants, some in desperate search for food and supplies, while others seized an opportunity to steal merchandise. At the same time, millions watched the horrific events unfold and wondered how camera crews and news commentators had reached the city while federal and state relief organizations failed to bring assistance. Former Louisiana senator John Breaux labeled the city "Baghdad under water." In hospitals, homes, shelters, and the streets, corpses began to pile up.

Dealing with the Damage

Rescue efforts were stymied by miscommunication, procedural red tape, and lack of preparation and resources. Mayor C. Ray Nagin of New Orleans, in a radio interview, blasted the federal government for its slow response, though the city's evacuation plans and state-level response had also been woefully inadequate. Nagin commanded the police force to abandon rescue missions and devote their time to stopping looters. Five hundred poorly trained National Guardsmen had maintained tenuous order with irresponsible threats at the

> Some critics accused Bush of callously allowing New Orleans to drown.

shelters. Anger and resentment grew as people began to feel forgotten and abused. In Washington, D.C., Secretary of Defense Donald Rumsfeld was hesitant to take the lead on disaster relief, something that was typically left to the National Guard and Federal Emergency Management Agency (FEMA). The Bush administration debated the legalities of who was in charge for days, while circumstances in New Orleans and the broader Gulf Coast region deteriorated. By the end of the week, a fleet of helicopters began to rescue survivors and drop off supplies, guardsmen brought food and water, and FEMA attempted to orchestrate transportation, but a centralized effort would not become apparent for several more days. Incredulous pundits questioned how a country that had taken pride in a new sense of preparedness following 9/11 had failed to mobilize after the storm. Further complicating the relief effort, more than 500,000 people had left the city. More people were displaced in a matter of days than had fled the Dust Bowl [a severe drought affecting the American Midwest] in the 1930s, and many had little hope of returning in the near future.

Relief Efforts

A week after the storm hit, troops and supplies, at last, poured into the city. The Superdome and the convention center, symbols of the city's desperation, were emptied, and survivors were bused out of New Orleans. A central

A residential area of Gulfport, Mississippi, lies in ruins on August 30, 2005, after being hit by high winds and tidal waves during Hurricane Katrina. (© **Paul J. Richards/AFP/Getty Images.**)

command station and medical triage were set up at the airport. With relief underway, politicians argued over whom to blame. Some critics accused Bush of callously allowing New Orleans to drown, pointing out that he had flown over the city on an unrelated trip and had failed to visit the city for five days. Both Democrats and Republicans expressed shock that Bush's senior staff had been unavailable, absent, or on holiday, and that Bush had remained aloof. Further, FEMA head Michael Brown offered little plausible explanation in defending the agency's slow and muddled response, while struggling nations—including Cuba, Sri Lanka, and Iran— had mobilized teams of doctors with food and medical supplies. Criticism of FEMA deepened when Homeland Security chief Michael Chertoff appeared on television claiming that he was unaware of people stranded at the Superdome, and reports revealed that Brown was ill-suited and unqualified for his position. The administration claimed that Hurricane Katrina was an unprecedented disaster that required a multifaceted and calculated response. Bush admonished attempts to politicize the tragedy, though he admitted that the government's relief efforts had been "unacceptable." His administration, however, maintained that state and local operations had failed and the federal government was merely helping to straighten out the mess.

> The worst flooding had disproportionately affected poor neighborhoods.

Criticism of the Response

The storm shook the faith of many Americans who waited in terror to be rescued or who helplessly watched thousands of people in New Orleans run out of safe water and food. A reported 1,600 people died. Many critics insisted that the government had failed to protect its citizens and began to ask why. For more than a century, the Army Corps of Engineers had shaped and reshaped the Mississippi River for commerce and constructed levees to protect from flooding. While conspiracy theories circulated that the Corps purposefully breached one levee in order to save New Orleans's wealthier enclaves, most agreed that inadequate funding and poor planning had crippled the city's flood protection. After [the al Qaeda–coordinated terrorist attacks of] 9/11, funds had overwhelmingly been redirected to national security. The worst flooding had disproportionately affected poor neighborhoods, just as the poor, elderly, and sick had suffered while others escaped. For New Orleans, like many American cities, the poorest citizens were also African American. Outraged critics claimed that racial discrimination had skewed media coverage and hampered rescue efforts. They argued that America's image had been weakened by the inequality exposed by the tragedy and called for efforts to reexamine racism. In all, 1.5 million people left New Orleans, sparking a massive demographic shift, largely absorbed by cities such as nearby Houston and Baton Rouge. New Orleans faced years of rebuilding its infrastructure and experimenting with environmental, cultural, and social policies. Other cities and states that sustained terrible damage bristled at the attention that New Orleans received. The impact of Hurricane Katrina continued to be felt in politics, sparking debates on race relations and discrimination, poverty, education, the effectiveness of federal and state emergency operations, and the difference between man-made and natural disasters.

Old West Has Nothing on Katrina Aftermath

Brian Thevenot, Keith Spera, and Doug MacCash

In the following viewpoint from August 31, 2005, journalists in New Orleans report on the effects of Hurricane Katrina in the immediate wake of the storm. Floodwaters continue to rise, the authors write, and the remaining residents in New Orleans are stranded in the city. The survivors of the storm face a lack of resources, dangerous flood conditions, and an increasingly lawless environment. In the midst of the calamity, the mayor of New Orleans says that another surge of water is expected from a failed levee. At the time the viewpoint was written, Brian Thevenot, Keith Spera, and Doug MacCash were staff writers for the New Orleans *Times-Picayune*.

Sitting on a black barrel amid the muck and stench near the St. Claude Avenue bridge, 52-year-old Daniel Weber broke into a sob, his voice cracking as he recounted how he had watched his wife drown and spent the next 14 hours floating in the polluted flood waters, his only life line a piece of driftwood.

"My hands were all cut up from breaking through the window, and I was standing on the fence. I said, 'I'll get on the roof and pull you up,'" he said. "And then we just went under."

Weber sat among hundreds of refugees rescued Tuesday from rooftops, attics and floating debris in the 9th Ward and St. Bernard Parish by an armada of more than 100 boats. Officials from the Coast Guard estimated they pulled thousands of people off of rooftops and attics, many with stories as grim as Weber's. Officials believed hundreds and maybe thousands more remained in peril. They declined to estimate the number of dead. That will come later.

"We've got cadaver dogs, but we're only looking for the live people at this point," said Rachel Zechnelli of the Department of Wildlife and Fisheries, which deployed all available boats to the Industrial Canal Monday night. "We're dealing only with live voices and heartbeats."

While the 9th Ward remained the focus of the search and rescue effort, refugees from other neighborhoods flooded by the massive breach of Lake Pontchartrain streamed to the Superdome and CBD [Central Business District], trudging through deep waters to get there.

Then, in an evening press conference, Mayor Ray Nagin announced that the already crippled city would take yet another blow: Another surge of water from the failed 17th Street Canal levee could push an additional 10 feet of water into already waterlogged neighborhoods, flooding the remaining dry sections of Uptown.

The expected surge stems from a failure to execute a plan to dump sandbags via helicopter into the 200-meter

New Orleans Prisoners Were Trapped by Floodwaters

On Monday, August 29 [2005], floodwaters began to enter the lower levels of the OPP [Orleans Parish Prison] buildings. According to one prisoner on the bottom floor of the Old Parish Prison, "we had water past our feet at the time, they [the deputies] gave us brooms and told us sweep the water out the cells." On the first floor of [prison building] Conchetta, deputies ordered one prisoner "to use a squeegie and pushbroom to push rising water of ground floor coming from outside and from inside sewer drains. It was futile. I looked for sandbags thinking we would use those for doorways and saw none." Another prisoner in South White Street reports that as a janitor/floor worker, or "Yank," he was ordered to place sandbags to prevent water from entering the building. Once that was done, he returned to his unit, where he remained until water began flooding his cell the next day.

On the first floor of [prison building] Templeman II, prisoners saw water seeping into the dorm through drainage holes in the floor. According to one prisoner, they began "sweeping the water under the door, in order to get the water from out the tier. . . . Unfortunately that didn't work, water continue to rise. Before I knew it my bottom bunk was underneath water. At this point I knew for sure the deputies was nowhere in the building. Still time continue to pass by, water still rising. No food for us to eat. Finally a female deputy came by we shouted to her about our conditions. She then replied there's nothing we can do because there's water everywhere and she left. At this point water had risen to at least 4 ft deep. I thought for sure I would never see freedom again."

Many of the women in Templeman IV were being held on minor offenses such as prostitution or simple drug possession. Templeman IV contains dormitory-style housing units with triple-stacked bunk beds. When water began to enter the building, it quickly rose to chest-level, forcing the women to climb onto the second and third levels of their bunks. One female prisoner reports: "[w]omen were made to urinate and defecate over the sides of the beds into the water; the water was *well* over the toilet seats."

SOURCE. *American Civil Liberties Union National Prison Project, "Abandoned and Abused: Orleans Parish Prisoners in the Wake of Hurricane Katrina," August 2006. www.aclu.org.*

wide breach. Nagin offered up no culprit but promised to investigate the matter.

"I thought everyone understood this morning that that was the highest priority," the mayor said. "It didn't get done. Now there's nothing to slow down the pace of the water."

That was enough to prompt some of the city's few remaining residents to start packing.

Uptown resident Margeaux Gonzalez rode out Katrina at the Queen and Crescent Hotel, then returned to find her Laurel Street home dry. As she and her neighbors watched Nagin on Tuesday night on a TV rigged to a car battery, they reluctantly made plans to evacuate to Baton Rouge.

> 'It's ridiculous that we can't get the help we need from the government to keep the city intact.'

"We were feeling really positive three hours ago," Gonzales said. "The storm is long gone, we suffered through the wind and the rain and survived the flood. It's ridiculous that we can't get the help we need from the government to keep the city intact. That's sad."

Earlier in the day, as floodwaters rose to knee-deep levels along Poydras Street, the city's top brass evacuated to Baton Rouge via the Crescent City Connection, the only clear route out of town. They recommended others follow.

"Get out," said City Attorney Sherry Landry from the window of the SUV she would use to evacuate. "I'm serious."

For many, that wasn't an option. In the impoverished 9th Ward, many didn't flee the storm in the first place because of lack of money and transportation, as well as a belief the storm wouldn't be nearly as bad. On Tuesday, they remained the focus of efforts to evacuate the homeless to the already crowded Superdome.

That left thousands of people in other neighborhoods close to the lake, whose homes had not flooded until late

Monday when the canal gave way, with no option other than to walk to the few dry areas of the city. Interstate 10 remained largely devoid of cars, but a steady stream of pedestrians seeking food, water and shelter walked along the highway.

More than 100 New Orleans police officers riding out the storm in the LSU Medical Center were still trapped by high water on Tuesday. Assumption Parish deputies in boats rescued them.

Some who left their flooded homes faced heart-rending dilemmas. Bethaney Waith of Mid-City, who walked in chest high water with a neighbor to the Superdome, had to leave her disabled housemate behind. The woman suffered from epidemia and can't walk.

> [A resident] started his own security patrol, driving around in his Ford pickup with his newly purchased handgun.

Those trapped in the city faced an increasingly lawless environment, as law enforcement agencies found themselves overwhelmed with widespread looting. Looters swarmed the Wal-Mart on Tchoupitoulas Street, often bypassing the food and drink section to steal wide-screen TVs, jewelry, bicycles and computers. Watching the sordid display and shaking his head in disgust, one firefighter said of the scene: "It's a hurricane, what are you [going to] do with a basketball goal?"

Police regained control at about 3 PM, after clearing the store with armed patrol. One shotgun-toting Third District detective described the looting as "ferocious."

"And it's going to get worse as the days progress," he said.

In Uptown, one of the few areas that remained dry, a bearded man patrolled Oak Street near the boarded-up Maple Leaf Bar, a sawed-off shotgun slung over his shoulder. The owners of a hardware store sat in folding chairs, pistols at the ready.

Uptown resident Keith Williams started his own security patrol, driving around in his Ford pickup with his newly purchased handgun. Earlier in the day, Williams said he had seen the body of a gunshot victim near the corner of Leonidas and Hickory streets.

"What I want to know is why we don't have paratroopers with machine guns on every street," Williams said.

Like-minded Art Depodesta sat on the edge of a picnic table outside Cooter Brown's Bar, a chrome shotgun at his side loaded with red shells.

"They broke into the Shell station across the street," he said. "I walked over with my 12-gauge and shot a couple into the air."

The looters scattered, but soon after, another man appeared outside the bar in a pickup truck armed with a pistol and threatened Depodesta.

"I told him, 'Listen, I was in the Army and I will blow your ass off,'" Depodesta said. "We've got enough trouble with the flood."

> The scene called to mind a refugee camp in a Third World nation.

The man sped away.

"You know what sucks," Depodesta said. "The whole U.S. is looking at this city right now, and this is what they see."

In the Bywater, a supply store sported spray-painted signs reading "You Loot, I Shoot" and "You Bein Watched." A man seated nearby with a rifle in his lap suggested it was no idle threat. At the Bywater studio of Dr. Bob, the artist known for handpainted "Be Nice or Leave" signs, a less fanciful sentiment was painted on the wall: "Looters Will Be Shot. Dr. Bob."

As the afternoon faded, aggression filled the air on the neutral ground of Poland Avenue as well, as people grew increasingly frustrated with the rescue effort. Having already survived one nightmare, a woman with five children feared going to go to the Dome, saying that

A policeman stands guard on a flooded downtown New Orleans street on August 31, 2005. At the time, conditions were deteriorating in the hurricane-hit city for the thousands of residents who had not been able to evacuate. (© Mario Tama/ Getty Images.)

some of the men preparing to board transport vehicles had smuggled razor blades with them.

On the other side of the bridge, rescue boats continued to offload as many as 15 people at a time late into the afternoon, with no end in sight. Some said they had seen dead bodies floating by their boats.

Many stumbled from dehydration as they made their way onto dry land. Several rescue workers said some of the people trapped were so shell-shocked or stubborn they refused to leave their houses. "If you can figure that one out, let me know," said Oscar Dupree, a volunteer who had been trapped on a roof himself and returned to help save others.

The scene called to mind a refugee camp in a Third World nation.

Liquor flowed freely and tempers flared amid complaints about the pace of the relief effort, which seemed to overwhelm the agencies involved and the city's inability to contain floodwaters.

As they emerged from rescue boats, at times wobbling and speaking incoherently, many of the rescued seem stunned they had not died. Johnell Johnson of Marais street said she had been trapped on her roof "with a handicapped man with one damn leg."

Gerald Wimberly wept as he recounted his unsuccessful effort to help a young girl, who rescuers ultimately saved.

Dupree said he had seen a young man he knew drown. "I just couldn't get to him," he said. "I had to tell his people."

Weber, the man who lost his wife, seemed at the breaking point as he waited, surrounded by anger and filth, for a National Guard truck to ferry him to the Dome. After 14 hours of floating on a piece of wood, volunteers who knew him had fished him out.

"Another hour, I would have just let myself drown," he said.

A moment later, staring ahead to a bleak future without his wife, he said he almost wished he had.

"I'm not going to make it. I know I'm not."

The US Government Responds to Hurricane Katrina

Michael Chertoff

In the following viewpoint, a federal official provides an overview of the government's response to Hurricane Katrina. In a news briefing in the wake of the storm, he states that the government is leading one of the largest response efforts in US history. He details the national response plan, which gives his department the responsibility to coordinate federal response and recovery efforts. He also explains the stages of recovery after the hurricane and the responsibilities of federal, state, and local authorities. Michael Chertoff served as the secretary of the US Department of Homeland Security from 2005 to 2009.

SOURCE. Michael Chertoff, "Michael Chertoff Holds a Homeland Security News Briefing Regarding Hurricane Katrina," Political/ Congressional Transcript Wire, August 31, 2005. Copyright © 2005 Political/Congressional Transcript Wire. All rights reserved. Reproduced with permission.

US Secretary of Homeland Security Michael Chertoff: The federal government is continuing to lead one of the largest response mobilizations in United States history to aid those who have had their homes and their lives devastated by Hurricane Katrina and its aftermath.

Our thoughts and prayers are with those who have lost loved ones and who continue to suffer in the aftermath of the storm.

We will work tirelessly to ensure that our fellow citizens have the sustained support and the necessary aid to recover and reclaim their homes, their lives and their communities.

President [George W.] Bush has declared major disasters for affected areas in Louisiana, Mississippi, Florida and Alabama. Along with these declarations, the full range of federal resources and capabilities is being directed, as we speak, to assist and protect those citizens who have borne the brunt of this catastrophe.

> We are extremely pleased with the response . . . of the federal government . . . to this terrible tragedy.

The Department of Homeland Security [DHS] has declared this an incident of national significance, the first-ever use of this designation under the new national response plan.

The national response plan, which was stood up earlier this year [2005], gives the Department of Homeland Security the lead responsibility to coordinate federal response and recovery efforts. The plan is designed to bring together all federal resources, to increase our ability to quickly get relief to those who need it most.

We are extremely pleased with the response that every element of the federal government, all of our federal partners, have made to this terrible tragedy. . . .

The situation in all the affected areas remains very dangerous. We want to emphasize that citizens should

The US Secretary of Homeland Security, Michael Chertoff (left), arrives in Baton Rouge, Louisiana, on September 5, 2005, with President George W. Bush and Lt. General Russel L. Honoré, the commander in charge of coordinating the military's efforts in Hurricane Katrina–affected areas. (© AP Images/ Lawrence Jackson.)

follow the instructions of state and local authorities who have asked that people remain in shelters and stay away from impacted areas until further notice. . . .

Assessing FEMA's Efforts

Let me first touch on those efforts undertaken through the Department of Homeland Security and its principal representative on the ground, FEMA [Federal Emergency Management Agency].

FEMA has deployed 39 disaster medical assistance teams from all across the United States to staging areas in Alabama, Tennessee, Texas and Louisiana. We are now moving them into impacted areas to provide emergency medical assistance.

FEMA's also moving supplies and equipment into the hardest-hit areas as quickly as possible—truckloads of water, ice, meals, medical supplies, generator, tents and tarpaulins. There are currently over 1,700 trailer trucks which have been mobilized to move these supplies into position.

The Coast Guard has worked heroically for the last 48 hours, rescuing or assisting well more than 1,000 people who were in distress and held high and dry above the flood waters.

I want to commend their efforts and their willingness to put their lives in danger to help others.

In addition, Coast Guard ships, boats and aircraft continue to support FEMA, state and local authorities with rescue and recovery efforts which are continuing to go on.

The Coast Guard has activated three national strike teams to help in the removal of hazardous material. Ships and boats continue to support the national relief effort. . . .

The magnitude of this challenge is enormous, but the combined capabilities of all parts of the United States government represented here and at other agencies has been brought to bear. And the president has been unambiguous in his mandate that we leave no stone unturned and leave no effort unexhausted in proceeding to do whatever we can to rescue people, alleviate suffering and address this terrible tragedy.

> " The president has been unambiguous in his mandate that we leave no stone unturned and leave no effort unexhausted. "

Explaining the Stages of Recovery

We're going to take some questions. If you'd simply tell us who you'd like to address the question to, we'll ask that person to answer.

Question: Mr. Chertoff, for you: Can you give us some sense of what you and your colleagues think you have accomplished so far, given the great need down there? Is this just the teeny beginning? Are you halfway there? Is this a tenth, a lot more to come? What is your sense of that?

Chertoff: You have to look at this problem in stages. The first stage is, of course, life-saving. We have to make sure

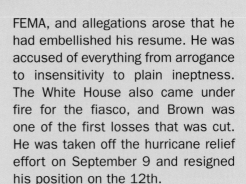

FEMA Director Michael Brown

Michael D. Brown was named head of the U.S. Federal Emergency Management Agency (FEMA) in 2003. Two years later, the embattled chief resigned amid an uproar over the agency's response to the devastating Hurricane Katrina, which struck New Orleans, Louisiana, in August of 2005. In the aftermath, it became apparent that the beleaguered Brown was out of his depth in the new position. . . . After Hurricane Katrina roared ashore, leaving vast destruction exacerbated by levees that did not hold and help that did not come, attention turned to the federal response. It was discovered that FEMA had delivered almost no assistance in the first 72 hours following the event. Indeed, the snafus, delays, and astonishing incompetence of the agency's rescue efforts shocked the world. And as the scandal escalated, Brown found himself at its nexus. Scrutiny of his background revealed no disaster experience outside of FEMA, and allegations arose that he had embellished his resume. He was accused of everything from arrogance to insensitivity to plain ineptness. The White House also came under fire for the fiasco, and Brown was one of the first losses that was cut. He was taken off the hurricane relief effort on September 9 and resigned his position on the 12th.

Whether Brown was entirely to blame for the debacle remained a subject of some debate. There were factions that saw his appointment as FEMA's chief to be the worst kind of political cronyism, and perceived the president as deflecting criticism that should have rightly been aimed at himself by pulling Brown off the job. Others saw Brown as the sole culprit. However, few disagreed that, whatever means were used to install Brown at FEMA's top, he was clearly not up to the task.

SOURCE. *"Michael Brown,"* Gale Biography in Context. *Detroit: Gale, 2005.*

we have found people who are at risk, either because of high winds or because of the flooding. We've got to locate them. We've got to rescue them.

I think we've made a lot of progress there. Well over 1,000 people have been rescued using Coast Guard helicopters. Boats manned by federal, state and local authorities have been out pulling people down from roofs. And there were people on a container, for example, that had to be rescued.

So we've made a lot of progress in that respect. A second piece of that initial rescue element involves what we have to do with evacuation. Again, we have made substantial progress there. There was a voluntary—actually, a mandatory evacuation before the storm hit. We are now positioning the assets necessary to evacuate the Superdome. We're going to do the other steps that are necessary to complete the evacuation.

So that's the first stage, and we're well into it.

A second stage is, obviously, going to be to then create the conditions that will allow people to shelter with food, water, safety for some period of time. We've got groups that are identifying locations for that, assembling the necessary materials. We've already indicated, for example, that those who are being evacuated from the Superdome will be going to Houston, to the Astrodome. That process is well along.

> "Under the Constitution, state and local authorities have the principal, first-line-of-response obligation, with respect to a disaster of this kind."

A third process which is probably [going to] take a longer period of time, is assessing the damage; dewatering, for example, those areas that have been flooded; evaluating what the condition of the infrastructure is and then seeing what steps need to be undertaken to repair and rebuild that infrastructure.

That is a longer time frame. We've begun that process. But I think that the time scale there is going to be measured in a longer, longer period. . . .

Recovery Is a Team Effort

In this first use of the law, are you in charge of local and state officials? And if there's any conflict between you and the locals and state, how does that get worked out? Also what's your relationship to the Defense Department in this?

Let me try to explain this. This shouldn't be news because it's in a plan that's been public for many months.

First of all, we come in to assist state and local authorities. Under the Constitution, state and local authorities have the principal, first-line-of-response obligation, with respect to a disaster of this kind.

Obviously, the law recognizes they can't do it themselves.

So we have a very detailed system of plans that allow us to work with them. We coordinate our response at DHS through FEMA.

Under the national response plan, all the departments of government play a role in the federal response to a disaster. DHS has the coordinating role or the managing role. The individual efforts that have to be undertaken—public health efforts, transportation efforts, energy efforts—are led by the individual departments of the federal government that have expertise in that area.

So it's a team effort. And like any team, everybody has a position to play. The head of the team is the president. And the president has, of course, the ultimate responsibility for all the federal effort here.

I can tell you the president is very deeply and personally involved in the details of what we're doing. We're going to be meeting with him later today. And, of course, again, I want to emphasize the federal government does not supersede the state and local government. We fit with the state and local government in a comprehensive response plan.

Mr. Secretary, how much have you spent so far or has the federal government spent so far on some of the recovery and relief? How much do you anticipate the entire effort will cost?

We're not keeping a running tally. I anticipate this is going to be a very, very substantial effort. I don't even think we have fully assessed all of the collateral consequences that are going to have to be dealt with. We have a substantial challenge but we do have some substantial resources. And we're going to do what it takes.

Do you have an estimate of—it's kind of related to this—a damage assessment in terms of how much it costs to how much—a financial damage assessment and the number of people that are dead?

> The process of getting our arms around the total cost is probably going to take a while.

In terms of the number of fatalities, there are unofficial estimates—there are official estimates. But I have to tell you that my sense is they are so— they will probably turn out not to be accurate by a considerable measure.

So I don't want to hazard a guess. In terms of the property damage, we're not going to know the full effect of this until we actually get in and look at what the consequences are on the ground.

You can look, yourself, at the pictures of large parts of New Orleans under water. And let me remind you that some of these areas include very expensive infrastructure. You have office buildings with cables, wire, a whole lot of underground piping which could be adversely affected.

We've got environmental cleanup issues here. There are issues of animal health. There are issues of public health.

So the process of getting our arms around the total cost is probably going to take a while.

This has been a devastating tragedy. And I think the impact of the hurricane on an urban area gives it a character that is a little different from the kinds of impacts we've seen in other areas.

They're all terrible. But the challenge when you deal particularly with the configuration of New Orleans and the surrounding parishes creates a special challenge because of the water and the flooding.

We're going to be, obviously, trying as quickly as possible to assess the total damage and develop a plan for doing what we need to do to repair and rebuild. But we're not going to have a definitive answer, I think, for a while.

States Welcome Hurricane Katrina Evacuees

Todd Lewan

In the following viewpoint, a journalist reports on the relocation of Gulf Coast residents dispossessed by Hurricane Katrina. Many of the evacuees have relocated to Texas, the author writes, and nearly a quarter-million people have filled the state's relief centers. He reports that numerous states have offered to help the storm victims and are putting programs in place to help those displaced. The author also details the efforts of volunteer groups and social service organizations that have helped evacuees find places to live, receive medical assistance, and find missing relatives. Todd Lewan is a journalist and author of *The Last Run: A True Story of Rescue and Redemption on the Alaska Seas*.

SOURCE. Todd Lewan, "States Welcome Refugees with Warm Hearts: 250,000 People Have Filled Centers in Texas," *St. Louis Post-Dispatch*, September 5, 2005. Copyright © 2010 St. Louis Post-Dispatch L.L.C. All rights reserved. Reproduced with permission.

With a shattered New Orleans all but emptied out, an unprecedented refugee crisis unfolded across the country Sunday [September 4, 2005], as governors and emergency officials struggled to feed, shelter and educate more than a half-million people dispossessed by Hurricane Katrina.

In Texas, where nearly a quarter-million refugees have filled the state's relief centers, Gov. Rick Perry ordered emergency officials to airlift some evacuees to other states willing to take them. Among the states that have offered help are Illinois, Missouri, West Virginia, Utah, Oklahoma, Michigan, Iowa, New York, West Virginia and Pennsylvania.

States Vow to Help the Evacuees

"There are shelters set up in other states that are sitting empty while thousands arrive in Texas by the day, if not the hour," Perry said. "To meet this enormous need, we need help from other states."

Around the country, social service agencies, businesses, volunteer groups, military bases and other refugee shelters rushed to set up procedures to help Katrina's dispossessed obtain their Social Security checks, receive their medicines, get their mail, find missing relatives and pets, and enroll their youngsters in school.

> Around the country, social service agencies, businesses, volunteer groups, military bases and other refugee shelters rushed . . . to help Katrina's dispossessed.

"We want to get the children back in school as quickly as possible, whether they are staying with relatives, or friends or in a shelter," said Caron Blanton, a spokeswoman for the Mississippi Department of Education. Mississippi, like Alabama, Florida, Texas and other states, has pledged to open its schools to displaced children and waive normal entry requirements like immunization records and proof of residency.

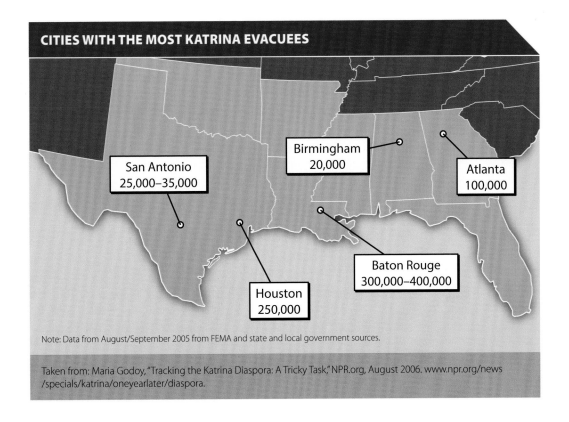

CITIES WITH THE MOST KATRINA EVACUEES

Birmingham
20,000

San Antonio
25,000–35,000

Atlanta
100,000

Baton Rouge
300,000–400,000

Houston
250,000

Note: Data from August/September 2005 from FEMA and state and local government sources.

Taken from: Maria Godoy, "Tracking the Katrina Diaspora: A Tricky Task," NPR.org, August 2006. www.npr.org/news /specials/katrina/oneyearlater/diaspora.

In Fort Chaffee, Ark., relief workers turned the post where Elvis Presley entered the Army in 1958 into a processing center for refugees. There, the homeless were registered by the Social Security Administration, checked by doctors and given post office boxes.

Marion Landry, 84, held onto the walker of her sister, Fay Roberts, 81, as the bedraggled pair went through the registration process. They appreciated the need for paperwork—but really wanted a shower.

"I've worn the same set of clothes for three days," said Roberts. "My hair is sweaty. I don't look like this. Normally I'm very nice."

Creating Welcome Stations

Meanwhile, a military base near Battle Creek, Mich., was transforming itself into a welcome station.

Thousands of people evacuated from Hurricane Katrina–affected areas fill the Astrodome in Houston, Texas, on September 3, 2005. (© Carlos Javier Sanchez/Bloomberg via Getty Images.)

Up to 500 evacuees were headed for the Fort Custer Training Center, where volunteer cooks were preparing meals at a mess hall normally for National Guard and military personnel from Ohio, Illinois and Indiana. Tables were stacked with towels, toiletries, T-shirts and other clothing and essentials. Medical personnel stood by to help, and clergy and attorneys were on call.

Michigan Gov. Jennifer Granholm said she would welcome the refugees to stay permanently, if they wished. "Michigan is going to welcome these victims, these evacuees, with open arms and show them some Northern hospitality," she said.

The National Center for Missing & Exploited Children, at the government's request, announced a hot line and Web site dedicated to reuniting family members separated by the storm. . . .

In New Mexico, Gov. Bill Richardson declared a state of emergency and released about $1 million to help victims of Hurricane Katrina as the first of up to 6,000 evacuees arrived Sunday. He also relaxed certain state transportation rules to speed up the building of temporary housing for the hurricane victims.

Refugees also began arriving in Arizona, which has agreed to take up to 2,500. They were greeted on the runway by Phoenix Mayor Phil Gordon.

> Carrying . . . their last belongings, the evacuees were led into the airport for physicals.

Several people had to be helped off the plane and down the stairway to the tarmac, where pink, yellow, teal and black flip-flops had been set out for them.

Then, carrying garbage bags, backpacks and brown shopping bags with their last belongings, the evacuees were led into the airport for physicals before boarding buses to the Veterans Memorial Coliseum.

"We'll take care of them," Gordon said. "We'll make sure they know that the city cares."

In Denver, Qwest Communications set up a bank of at least 50 phones at a processing center so refugees could call loved ones. Colorado state Rep. Debbie Stafford said she was trying to arrange long-term shelter, and also reunite some people with their pets.

State and local officials in Texas, Tennessee, Georgia and other states with a refugee influx began setting up programs to link refugees with employers. Business owners are trying to help, too.

In Richland, Miss., a fast-food restaurant hung fliers at a shelter offering jobs. A steel company sent employees to a shelter at the Mississippi Coliseum in Jackson to recruit new workers. And Craigslist, the Internet-based classified advertising service, was filled with job offers for people willing to relocate.

Evacuees Endure Horrible Conditions in the Louisiana Superdome

Scott Gold

In the following viewpoint, a journalist reports on the horrific conditions New Orleans residents suffered inside the Louisiana Superdome after Hurricane Katrina. The Superdome became the largest shelter in the New Orleans area, the author writes, and housed about sixteen thousand people after the storm. In the aftermath of the hurricane, the Superdome lost power, and those in the shelter were trapped without electricity in unsanitary conditions, he reports. There were few resources available, according to the author, and many of the evacuees were fearful of the violent environment inside the putative shelter. Scott Gold is a senior writer at the *Los Angeles Times*.

A 2-year-old girl slept in a pool of urine. Crack vials littered a restroom. Blood stained the walls next to vending machines smashed by teenagers.

The Louisiana Superdome, once a mighty testament to architecture and ingenuity, became the biggest storm shelter in New Orleans the day before Katrina's arrival Monday [August 29, 2005]. About 16,000 people eventually settled in.

A Horrific Environment

By Wednesday, it had degenerated into horror. A few hundred people were evacuated from the arena Wednesday, and buses will take away the vast majority of refugees today [September 1, 2005].

"We pee on the floor. We are like animals," said Taffany Smith, 25, as she cradled her 3-week-old son, Terry. In her right hand she carried a half-full bottle of formula provided by rescuers. Baby supplies are running low; one mother said she was given two diapers and told to scrape them off when they got dirty and use them again.

> There is no sanitation. The stench is overwhelming.

At least two people, including a child, have been raped. At least three people have died, including one man who jumped 50 feet to his death, saying he had nothing left to live for.

The hurricane left most of southern Louisiana without power, and the arena, which is in the central business district of New Orleans, was not spared. The air conditioning failed immediately and a swampy heat filled the dome.

An emergency generator kept some lights on, but quickly failed. Engineers have worked feverishly to keep a backup generator running, at one point swimming under the floodwater to knock a hole in the wall to install a new diesel fuel line. But the backup generator is now faltering and almost entirely submerged.

There is no sanitation. The stench is overwhelming. The city's water supply, which had held up since Sunday, gave out early Wednesday, and toilets in the Superdome became inoperable and began to overflow.

"There is feces on the walls," said Bryan Hebert, 43, who arrived at the Superdome on Monday. "There is feces all over the place."

Soldiers Try to Help Despite Limited Resources

The Superdome is patrolled by more than 500 Louisiana National Guard troops, many of whom carry machine guns as sweaty, smelly people press against metal barricades that keep them from leaving, shouting as the soldiers pass by: "Hey! We need more water! We need help!"

Most refugees are given two 9-ounce bottles of water a day and two boxed meals: spaghetti, Thai chicken or jambalaya.

One man tried to escape Wednesday by leaping a barricade and racing toward the streets. The man was desperate, National Guard Sgt. Caleb Wells said. Everything he was able to bring to the Superdome had been stolen. His house had probably been destroyed, his relatives killed.

"We had to chase him down," Wells said. "He said he just wanted to get out, to go somewhere. We took him to the terrace and said: 'Look.'"

Below, floodwaters were continuing to rise, submerging cars.

"He didn't realize how bad things are out there," Wells said. "He just broke down. He started bawling. We took him back inside."

The soldiers—most are sleeping two or three hours a night, and many have lost houses—say they are doing the best they can with limited resources and no infrastructure. But they have become the target of many refugees' anger.

"They've got the impression that we have everything and they have nothing," 1st Sgt. John Jewell said. "I tell them: 'We're all in the same boat. We're living like you're living.' Some of them understand. Some of them have lost their senses."

Waiting for Help

Thousands of people are still wading to high ground out of the flooding, and most head for the Superdome. Officials have turned away hundreds.

"The conditions are steadily declining," said Maj. Ed Bush. "The systems have done all they can do. We don't know how much longer we can hold on. The game now is to squeeze everything we can out of the Superdome and then get out."

New Orleans Mayor C. Ray Nagin said Wednesday that more than 100 buses were staged outside the city for today's evacuation. He had asked officials in Baton Rouge and Lafayette, La., to send all of their school buses—about 500—to New Orleans. If all of the buses make it into the city, Nagin said, the Superdome could be cleared out by nightfall today.

> 'People started shooting last night.'

Most of the people will go to Houston, where they will stay in the Astrodome. Others will be taken to Louisiana cities that escaped the hurricane.

Between 400 and 500 people, many with critical medical conditions, were airlifted or bused Wednesday from the sports complex; some were taken to Houston.

"They need to see psychologically that this is real," Nagin said. "They need to see that they are really moving. They need to see people getting on the bus. I want to start to create a sense of hope."

That will be difficult. There is a local legend that sports teams that have called the Superdome home have fared poorly because the facility, which broke ground in 1971, was built atop a cemetery. Perhaps, some said Wednesday, the curse is real.

Inside, a man coughed up blood and his shoulders quaked as he was wheeled through the halls. Thousands clutched their meager belongings, sitting in seats normally used for football games or lying on the artificial turf, its end zones painted with the word "Saints."

Residents Fear for Their Lives

Some slept out on the terrace, trying to get shade under a National Guard truck. Young boys who had lost their shoes hopped on the hot pavement to save their scalding feet. Grown men discarded their clothes and walked around in their briefs.

"People started shooting last night," said Stacey Bodden, 11.

Bodden and six relatives fled their homes in the West Bank—which survived the storm in relatively good condition—to ride out the storm in the Superdome. By Wednesday evening, the family had had enough and was going to try to get out and walk home through the floodwater and across the Crescent City Connection, a massive bridge spanning the Mississippi River.

> Some people had wrapped plastic bags on their feet to escape the urine and wastewater seeping from piles of trash.

Her uncle David Rodriguez, 28, said he heard at least seven shots Tuesday night and saw one man running past him with a gun. "Don't shoot," he told the man, who didn't.

"This is a nuthouse," said April Thomas, 42, who fled to the Superdome with her 11 children. She has enlisted the older boys to take turns walking patrols at night as the rest of the family sleeps.

"You have to fend people off constantly," she said. "You have to fight for your life. I wake up in the morn-

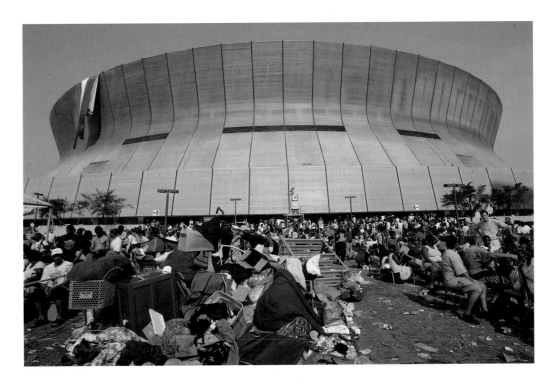

ing and the first thing I say is: Where are my babies? Is everyone here?"

There's a thriving black market; the most popular items are cigarettes, which sell for $10 a pack, and anti-diuretics, which allow people to avoid using the bathroom for as long as possible.

Many of the injured, the elderly and the critically ill, and those suffering from dehydration, have been taken across a walkway to an adjoining sports center, the New Orleans Arena.

One man was lying partway on a cot, his legs flopped off the side, a forgotten blood pressure monitor attached to his right arm. Some people had wrapped plastic bags on their feet to escape the urine and wastewater seeping from piles of trash. Others, fearing the onset of disease, had surgical masks over their mouths. An alarm had been going off for more than 24 hours and no one knew how to turn it off.

Residents of New Orleans wait to be rescued on September 2, 2005, outside the Superdome, where evacuees had experienced horrific and unsafe conditions. (© James Nielsen/AFP/Getty Images.)

Suddenly, incongruously, the first notes of Bach's Sonata No. 1 in G minor, the Adagio, pierced the desperation.

Samuel Thompson, 34, is trying to make it as a professional violinist. He had grabbed his instrument—made in 1996 by a Boston woman—as he fled the youth hostel Sunday where he had been staying in New Orleans for the last two months.

"It's the most important thing I own," he said.

He had guarded it carefully and hadn't taken it out until Wednesday afternoon, when he was able to move from the Superdome into the New Orleans Arena, far safer accommodations. He rested the black case on a table next to a man with no legs in a wheelchair and a pile of trash and boxes, and gingerly popped open the two locks. He lifted the violin out of the red velvet encasement and held it to his neck.

Thompson closed his eyes and leaned into each stretch of the bow as he played mournfully. A woman eating crackers and sitting where a vendor typically sold pizza watched him intently. A National Guard soldier applauded quietly when the song ended, and Thompson nodded his head and began another piece, the Andante from Bach's Sonata in A minor.

Thompson's family in Charleston, S.C., has no idea where he is and whether he is alive. Thompson figures he is safe for now and will get in touch when he can. In the meantime he will play, and once in a while someone at the sports complex will manage a smile.

"These people have nothing," he said. "I have a violin. And I should play for them. They should have something."

Hurricane Katrina Causes Extensive Environmental Damage

Erik D. Olson

In the following viewpoint, a representative of the Natural Resources Defense Council (NRDC) presents a report on the environmental damage caused by Hurricane Katrina. There has been a widespread release of raw sewage, petroleum, and other toxins in the Gulf Coast, the author states. The NRDC is concerned that residents are returning to toxic areas throughout the region without the proper protections, which could lead to widespread illnesses, as the region is repopulated. The organization examines the short-term and potential long-term effects of what it concludes is one of the worst environmental disasters in US history. Erik D. Olson is the senior strategic director for health and food at the Natural Resources Defense Council.

Katrina is perhaps the single worst environmental catastrophe ever to befall the United States as a result of a natural disaster. Having just observed the extraordinary devastation of this calamity—as exacerbated by the subsequent Hurricane Rita—it is difficult to express the stunning and deeply moving extent of the human tragedy that has been left in its wake.

We saw thousands of homes devastated by the water; walls imploded, thick layers of sediment strewn inside and out, mold coating the interior of the homes, roofs collapsed, and some homes picked up by the water and moved into the middle of streets. Thousands of vehicles—cars, trucks and buses—were completely or largely submerged and destroyed and are sprinkled in unexpected locations across the area, many left precariously leaning up against roofs, teetering on fences, stacked on top of each other, or crushed by the powerful water. Entire commercial strips were completely destroyed, schools and public buildings wrecked, power lines toppled including toxics-laden transformers, and gas stations ruined. The hard-hit areas were largely ghost towns, but in recent days, thousands of people are beginning to return.

> The strong smell of petroleum vapors is frequently encountered, as are the stench of putrefying sludge and organic matter, and . . . mold.

The smell is overpowering in many areas. The strong smell of petroleum vapors is frequently encountered, as are the stench of putrefying sludge and organic matter, and the unmistakable odor of widespread mold. Dust swirls into your lungs when heavy equipment moves or a breeze kicks it up, as the muck has largely dried into a broken layer of dark residue from half an inch to several inches or more deep.

As any of the brave and stalwart citizens of Louisiana, Mississippi, and Alabama who survived Hurricane Katrina will tell you, this disaster has left an indelible mark on them and their families, communities, and environment. The loss of human life and widespread human misery that Katrina caused and continues to cause as we sit in this room today, are simply unfathomable.

This testimony will focus on the environmental effects of Katrina—and in particular on the potential effects of toxins in the storm-ravaged area. Specifically, I intend to focus primarily on the known and potential human health effects of the widespread releases of raw sewage, petroleum, and other toxins into the environment.

Reports of Severe Pollution and Illnesses

We are receiving regular, albeit anecdotal, reports of police, rescue workers, and ordinary people who have returned to or stayed in flooded areas and have become ill after contact with the flood water or muck. Reports of rashes and blisters where skin has contacted polluted water, infected sores that are not responsive to antibiotics, nausea, and vomiting are legion. Respiratory problems—including asthma among many people exposed to fumes in contaminated areas—also are being reported.

One woman's brother returned to his home to try to recover a few belongings, only to vomit three times upon entering the home due to the stench of sewage, decay, and chemicals. I spoke to the mother of a young man who wore hip waders into floodwaters, but whose skin came in contact with the toxic water. The same day, he developed a rash and blisters where his skin had touched the water. We have heard from many local citizens about police officers and other emergency workers who have come into contact with the polluted flood water, only to develop rashes and other symptoms. The long-term effects of this toxic exposure are unknown, and of profound concern to us and to many local citizens.

> People returning home do not have ready access to emergency medical services.

One public health nurse working with the Red Cross spoke to us and reported that she had seen, by her count, over a thousand evacuees in Mississippi, but she had no tetanus or hepatitis vaccine to give to evacuees who were planning to return home to their water-soaked communities.

We observed in our tour of hard-hit areas that as the floodwater has receded, and the toxin-laced sediment and residue has dried, dust begins to swirl with wind or disturbance. This fine, toxic dust presents a serious risk to citizens if inhaled.

In many of the hardest-hit areas, people returning home do not have ready access to emergency medical services, nor to nearby health clinics, physicians, or hospital emergency rooms. While improving, communications also remain difficult in many areas. It is therefore difficult to determine how widespread and serious these problems are, but it is likely that many people are suffering without appropriate medical care. There is an urgent need for better-coordinated and more comprehensive medical care and for ongoing disease surveillance by the

A photo from August 31, 2005, shows toxic chemicals in the floodwaters around an oil and gas facility in Louisiana that was damaged during Hurricane Katrina. (© Scott Saltzman/Bloomberg via Getty Images.)

Centers for Disease Control and Prevention or Agency for Toxic Substances Disease Registry.

There are enormous health hazards from the toxic residue and floodwaters. Contact with remaining water poses a serious risk of waterborne disease. Widespread petroleum spills and leaks have caused extensive and health-threatening air and water pollution, and as the heavy metal and other pollutant-laden residue in many areas from the flood dries and becomes airborne dust, it poses additional risks when inhaled.

Spills and Leaks of Oil and Toxic Chemicals

According to U.S. Coast Guard and EPA [US Environmental Protection Agency] data, as of September 18, [2005,] 575 Katrina-related spills of petroleum or hazardous chemical had been reported. Just eleven significant spills released approximately 7 million gallons of oil, a portion of which was contained or cleaned up, but much of which was not.

We also understand that there are 350,000 or more ruined automobiles and other vehicles caught by the flooding that will have to be dealt with. The amount of gasoline and toxic fluids in these vehicles alone is enough to give one pause; if each gas tank contained approximately 8 gallons of gasoline, this adds nearly 3 million additional gallons to the 7 million-gallon total noted above. By comparison, 11 million gallons of oil were released in the Exxon Valdez disaster [a 1989 oil spill in Alaska].

Moreover, at least four Superfund hazardous waste sites in the New Orleans area were hit by the storm. Across the storm-ravaged areas of Louisiana, Mississippi, and Alabama dozens of other toxic waste sites, major industrial facilities, ports, barges, and vessels that handle enormous quantities of oil and hazardous chemicals took a direct blow from Katrina.

In addition to oil and chemical spills, and potential releases from toxic waste or industrial facilities, one major source of toxins that has received very little public attention to date is the toxic sediment that has accumulated at the bottom of many of the lakes, rivers, and streams in industrialized areas over many decades due to industrial spills. These toxic underwater hotspots have long been of concern to state and federal officials. According to experts with whom we have spoken in Louisiana, many of these toxic hotspots have now been stirred up, and toxic sediment has been re-suspended, and re-deposited across large land areas, including in residential communities, by storm surge and floodwater.

> EPA has released air monitoring data . . . showing that contaminants are at unsafe levels for rehabitating certain parts of the city.

To date, virtually no public information is available about toxic chemical levels in areas outside of [the] New Orleans area. Moreover, there have been virtually no public reports of the results of chemical testing or inspections of storm-damaged industrial facilities outside of this immediate area.

Dangerous Levels of Air Contamination

Agency data also show that elevated levels of toxic chemicals such as benzene and xylene, in some cases levels above the 24-hour safety limits, have been found in the air adjacent to spills.

Perhaps more troublingly, EPA has released air monitoring data from its Trace Atmospheric Gas Analyser (TAGA) buses and other monitors used across New Orleans, showing that contaminants are at unsafe levels for rehabitating certain parts of the city. NRDC [Natural Resources Defense Council] has reached this conclusion by comparing benzene monitoring results, posted on EPA's website, to levels that the National Institute of Environmental Health Sciences (NIEHS) established to protect people from intermediate-term (e.g., two-week) exposures to this chemical—a level of 4 ppb. Significantly, in 25% of the areas sampled in New Orleans, EPA monitoring shows levels of benzene more than twice this NIEHS intermediate safety level. Yet EPA's charts and discussions on its website only compare elevated air pollution levels to the much higher (50 ppb) acute NIEHS safety level—that is, to a level that is only considered safe for very short-term (e.g., 24-hour) exposure. Moreover, no air or other sampling has been publicly reported for most areas around spills or chemical facilities outside of New Orleans.

> "We saw many citizens returning to petroleum or other toxin-tainted areas, generally using no masks or special protective clothing."

Despite the inadequacy of these test results, EPA asserts in its public materials that, "[t]he screening results indicated that chemical concentrations in most areas are below ATSDR [Agency for Toxic Substances and Disease Registry] health standards of concern." These kinds of agency statements have undoubtedly led to widespread confusion and may have misled the public and local officials about the safety of returning to polluted areas.

Citizens and Responders Do Not Understand the Seriousness of the Risks

In light of the lack of adequate and accurate public information, people are returning to toxin-soaked areas without understanding the risks, and without being provided the proper protections, warnings, or knowledge. We are extremely concerned that there may be widespread illnesses and toxic exposure effects as toxin-soaked areas are repopulated.

We saw many citizens returning to petroleum or other toxin-tainted areas, generally using no masks or special protective clothing. EPA data show that not only does air pollution present a risk, but fetid floodwater that remains in some pockets of the flooded area and still soaks the interiors of many homes and businesses contain high levels of bacteria and other waterborne pathogens from raw sewage, and in many areas contain elevated levels of petroleum, lead, and other toxins.

Many people—both ordinary citizens and emergency workers or police personnel—are breathing petroleum vapors, coming into contact with petroleum and other toxin-polluted water, debris, or residue, or cleaning up polluted homes and businesses, with little or no personal protection. Whereas contract cleanup workers donning Tyvek "moon suits" cleaned up oil and hazmat spills, the public generally is using no protection even though they may well experience dangerous levels of exposure. The National Contingency Plan and EPA and OSHA [Occupational Safety and Health Administration] regulations require that anyone working on response to an oil or hazardous substance spill be provided with appropriate protective gear, and contract cleanup workers are in some cases wearing protective gear. But from what we observed and according to reports we have received, many local police and other workers in the area are not wearing protection such as respirators and protective clothing.

Environmental Injustices Will Be Exacerbated

There is a longstanding legacy of unfair and disproportionate toxic exposures to low income, predominantly African American communities in the New Orleans area and in much of Louisiana, Mississippi, and Alabama. This has resulted from years of industrial activity and waste disposal practices that hit these communities far harder than higher income, predominantly white communities. TRI [Toxics Release Inventory] and Superfund facilities are located more often in low income areas and

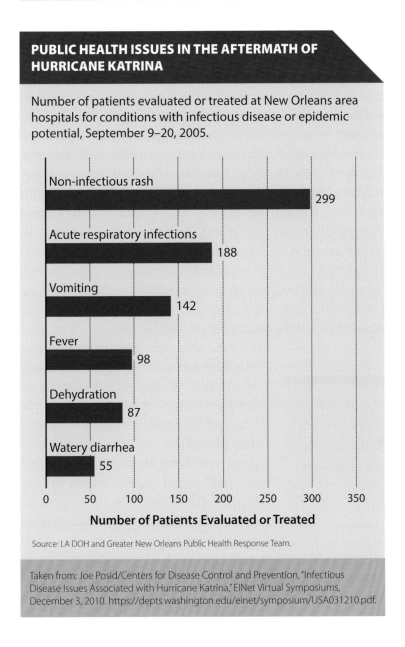

PUBLIC HEALTH ISSUES IN THE AFTERMATH OF HURRICANE KATRINA

Number of patients evaluated or treated at New Orleans area hospitals for conditions with infectious disease or epidemic potential, September 9–20, 2005.

Non-infectious rash — 299

Acute respiratory infections — 188

Vomiting — 142

Fever — 98

Dehydration — 87

Watery diarrhea — 55

Number of Patients Evaluated or Treated

Source: LA DOH and Greater New Orleans Public Health Response Team.

Taken from: Joe Posid/Centers for Disease Control and Prevention, "Infectious Disease Issues Associated with Hurricane Katrina," EINet Virtual Symposiums, December 3, 2010. https://depts.washington.edu/einet/symposium/USA031210.pdf.

therefore are at greater risk to post-Katrina exposure. As cleanup proceeds and rebuilding begins, every effort must be made to remedy these environmental injustices through full cleanup, fair rebuilding practices, and full partnership with affected communities.

Toxics Testing Must Be Expanded

EPA has released a limited amount of water, sediment, and air testing for the New Orleans area. There are literally hundreds of reported oil and toxics spills, industrial waste dumps, and industrial facilities that handle substantial quantities of toxic chemicals across Louisiana, Mississippi, and Alabama that were hit hard by Katrina, but for which there has been no reported toxics testing.

In addition, even in those areas around New Orleans that were tested, often only a few samples have been reported for most locations, triggering concern that as water receded or came in from other locations, as re-flooding from Rita occurred, as leaks or spills spread, as waste leached, or as other conditions changed, toxic levels were likely to change as well, likely leaving toxic residues in many locations across the area.

> Information [should be disseminated] through the mainstream media about the toxics threats and the need to take appropriate precautions.

We also are deeply concerned that EPA has delayed reporting many of its test results. As hundreds of thousands of people are returning to evacuated communities, it is critical that EPA release its data immediately upon receiving them, to assure that the public and local officials are informed about the risks.

In addition, we have heard from many local citizens and some local elected officials that EPA's method of releasing most test results—on the web—is not an effective way to get information to the vast majority of evacuees who do not have Internet access and are often not able to digest and understand the data. EPA and CDC's [US Centers for Disease Control and Prevention] press conference warning of the risks of coming into contact with the flood waters was helpful, but came so long ago that it is for many a distant memory that does not touch upon the hazards today from the soaked homes and debris, sediments, mold and other toxins citizens are likely to encounter as they return.

The lack of regular, understandable, and repeatedly-reiterated information through the mainstream media about the toxics threats and the need to take appropriate precautions (e.g. rubber boots, Tyvek suits, masks or respirators, impermeable gloves) is likely to lead to continued widespread misunderstandings and health threats.

Officials Have "Punted" Their Responsibility

EPA is the nation's primary repository of expertise and regulatory and enforcement authority for controlling and responding to environmental toxin threats to the public's health. As such, the agency must assume the responsibility for assuring, after the massive spills and releases of oil and hazardous substances in the wake of Katrina, that the health of citizens living in or returning to the affected communities is fully protected.

Ray Nagin Is 17th N.O.-Area Politician Sentenced Since Katrina

Gordon Russell

In the following viewpoint, a journalist reports on the conviction of former New Orleans mayor Ray Nagin in July 2014. Nagin, who served as mayor of New Orleans during Hurricane Katrina, was sentenced on federal corruption charges for illegal dealings with city vendors. The author writes that Nagin is the seventeenth New Orleans–area elected official sentenced on corruption charges after Hurricane Katrina. He attributes the rise in convictions to local coalitions that formed after the storm in an effort to fight corruption. Gordon Russell is managing editor of investigations at the *New Orleans Advocate*.

When Ray Nagin is sentenced Wednesday, he'll become the first New Orleans mayor to face prison time for selling his office.

The punishment he'll endure—which could be as much as two decades in prison—may be the stiffest sentence any local politician has received in a corruption case. But the spectacle of another crooked Crescent City politician being sent off to the federal pen is hardly an unusual one.

In fact, Nagin, 58, will become the 17th elected official from the city and its suburbs to be sentenced on federal corruption or fraud charges since Hurricane Katrina laid waste to the region nine years ago.

> The parade of shame includes politicians at almost every level, from [almost] every parish in the metropolitan area.

The parade of shame includes politicians at almost every level, from every parish in the metropolitan area except for St. Charles. It includes a congressman, two parish presidents, a sheriff, a coroner, a judge, an assessor, a state representative, a state senator, a school board member, four members of city councils, a parish council member and two mayors.

It's hard to explain the crush of cases. While New Orleans, perhaps unfairly, has always been known as a place where a flexible sense of morality has never been an impediment to political success, the city has never seen such an avalanche of corruption convictions.

There's little to tie the various cases together save for greed. Certainly, there's little evidence to support the notion that the region's politicians lost their collective moral compass in the wake of the storm, and some of the crimes they've been convicted of predate Katrina.

But some of the cases can be traced to an energized, and often outraged, citizenry that was finally fed up with the old ways. The storm—and the endless, sometimes contentious meetings that followed it—helped to create

A Police Department Indifferent to the Rule of Law

The NOPD [New Orleans Police Department] has long been a troubled agency. Basic elements of effective policing—clear policies, training, accountability, and confidence of the citizenry—have been absent for years. Far too often, officers show a lack of respect for the civil rights and dignity of the people of New Orleans. While the majority of the force is hardworking and committed to public safety, too many officers of every rank either do not understand or choose to ignore the boundaries of constitutional policing. Some argue that, given the difficulty of police work, officers must at times police harshly and bend the rules when a community is confronted with seemingly intransigent high levels of crime. Policing is undeniably difficult; however, experience and study in the policing field have made it clear that bending the rules and ignoring the Constitution makes effective policing much more challenging. NOPD's failure to ensure that its officers routinely respect the Constitution and the rule of law undermines trust within the very communities whose cooperation the Department most needs to enforce the law and prevent crime. As systematic violations of civil rights erode public confidence, policing becomes more difficult, less safe, and less effective, and crime increases.

The deficiencies in the way NOPD polices the City are not simply individual, but structural as well. For too long, the Department has been largely indifferent to widespread violations of law and policy by its officers. NOPD does not have in place the basic sys-

coalitions that fought to consolidate the region's fractured levee boards, unify the city's assessment operations and create a strong and independent inspector general's office.

"It was life-changing," said real estate agent Ruthie Frierson, who after the storm became the face of Citizens for 1 Greater New Orleans, a group that mobilized to push various reforms. "There was citizen engagement like never before. What people saw (in the storm's aftermath) was a frightful sight. And it made everyone recognize we needed change, and we needed to be engaged."

tems known to improve public safety, ensure constitutional practices, and promote public confidence. We found that the deficiencies that lead to constitutional violations span the operation of the entire Department, from how officers are recruited, trained, supervised, and held accountable, to the operation of Paid Details. In the absence of mechanisms to protect and promote civil rights, officers too frequently use excessive force and conduct illegal stops, searches and arrests with impunity. In addition, the Department's culture tolerates and encourages under-enforcement and under-investigation of violence against women. The Department has failed to take meaningful steps to counteract and eradicate bias based on race, ethnicity, and LGBT status in its polic-

ing practices, and has failed to provide critical policing services to language minority communities.

The problems in NOPD developed over a long period of time and will take time to address and correct. The Department must develop and implement new policies and protocols, train its officers in effective and constitutional policing, and institutionalize systems to ensure accountability, foster police-community partnerships, improve the quality of policing to all parts of the City, and eliminate unlawful bias from all levels of NOPD policing decisions.

SOURCE. *United States Department of Justice, Civil Rights Division, "Investigation of the New Orleans Police Department," March 16, 2011. www.justice.gov.*

Frierson said groups like hers made common cause with other leaders and organizations, from the Urban League and Court Watch NOLA to Women of the Storm, to demand better of the region's politicians.

Similar impulses may also have helped bring about some of the long list of criminal prosecutions of public officials that came after Katrina, directly and indirectly.

For instance, less than two months after the storm, when St. Tammany Parish Councilman Joe Impastato tried to set himself up to receive kickbacks from the owner of a debris-staging site, the owner, Lee Mauberret,

> **Fed-up residents also called newspapers and television stations to carp about abuses by their elected officials.**

went to the feds instead of playing ball. Mauberret wore a wire, and the FBI quickly put together a case against Impastato, who eventually pleaded guilty.

Fed-up residents also called newspapers and television stations to carp about abuses by their elected officials, spawning a wave of stories that led directly to federal investigations.

Among the politicians whose undignified ends had their beginnings with news reports: Eddie Price, the former Mandeville mayor; Renee Gill Pratt, the former New Orleans City Council member and state representative; Betty Jefferson, the former assessor for the city's 4th Municipal District; Peter Galvan, the former St. Tammany Parish coroner; and Nagin.

The role of the U.S. Attorney's Office also can't be overstated. Jim Letten, who was the longest-serving top prosecutor in the country when he resigned in late 2012, made his name by successfully prosecuting former Gov. Edwin Edwards. As U.S. attorney, he oversaw a probe into the contracting practices of former Mayor Marc Morial's administration that led to the convictions of several close Morial associates.

Letten's frequent news conferences touting indictments and convictions of politicians led some to criticize him as a publicity hound. But his focus on public corruption was undeniable, and it sent a message to the public that the feds were playing hardball.

The office, of course, has since been tarnished by the online-commenting scandal involving two of Letten's top lieutenants that eventually prompted Letten's own exit. But the convictions—at least those of public officials—have all stood up.

Kenneth Polite, who last year replaced Letten as U.S. attorney, has pledged he won't let up the fight on public corruption, though he has signaled a shift in the office's priorities, with a greater emphasis on combating violent crime. His office recently opened a grand-jury investigation into embattled longtime St. Tammany District Attorney Walter Reed.

> "It's almost inevitable that [Mayor Ray] Nagin will draw one of the longest sentences meted out."

Nagin's sentencing, in some ways, will mark the end of the Letten legacy, though the lead prosecutors in the case, Matt Coman and Richard Pickens, have taken pains to say that neither Letten nor either of his disgraced assistants was involved in the case.

It's almost inevitable that Nagin will draw one of the longest sentences meted out to any New Orleans-area politician brought down in the last decade. His attorney has indicated that a pre-sentence report prepared by federal probation officers calls for a sentence of 20 years at the low end. If U.S. District Judge Ginger Berrigan goes along with that recommendation, Nagin's punishment would be stiffer than that imposed on former Gretna City Councilman Jonathan Bolar, now serving a 17-year sentence on extortion and other charges.

The only other local politician in the same ballpark is former U.S. Rep. William Jefferson, who was sentenced to 13 years on bribery charges.

Bolar, Jefferson and Nagin have one thing in common: They all professed their innocence in the face of corruption charges, rolled the dice and went to trial.

CHAPTER 2

Controversies Surrounding Hurricane Katrina

Predictions That a Major Storm Would Devastate New Orleans Went Unheeded

Ivor van Heerden, interviewed by NOVA

In the following viewpoint, NOVA, a science documentary series, interviews a hurricane expert about his predictions prior to Hurricane Katrina. Hurricane forecasters warned government officials for years about the vulnerability of New Orleans to a major storm, the expert contends, but government officials were not responsive to the warnings and failed to make strengthening the levee system a priority. He maintains that government officials were warned days before Katrina hit that there would be major flooding in New Orleans, but they did not properly prepare evacuation plans—a failure that unnecessarily jeopardized lives and property. At the time of Hurricane Katrina, Ivor van Heerden was the deputy director of the Louisiana State University

Photo on opposite page: Floodwaters surround the Superdome in downtown New Orleans on August 30, 2005, in the aftermath of Hurricane Katrina. (© Marko Georgiev/Getty Images.)

Hurricane Center. He was interviewed by NOVA scienceNOW correspondent Peter Standring on September 10, 2005, and by NOVA producer Tom Stubberfield on October 5, 2005.

*N*OVA: *Bring me back: Katrina comes through Florida and starts making its way across the Gulf. Here at the Hurricane Center at LSU [Louisiana State University], what do you do?*

Ivor van Heerden: Early Saturday morning [August 27, 2005], we assembled at LSU and started doing the [storm surge] model runs. We did about three that day. And the last one we did we released in the evening, and that was the one that showed that New Orleans was actually going to flood. I then sent an e-mail to a lot of different federal agencies, state agencies, the media, letting them know what was happening.

> '[Our model] showed that most of eastern New Orleans was going to be underwater.'

The Weather Channel and then the [New Orleans] *Times-Picayune* contacted us, and they wanted to use it for an article for Sunday morning. So we worked with them to get that together, because we felt that the *Times-Picayune* could have a good image that might hasten the number of people who left. And obviously, we were doing whatever media interviews we could to get the message out: "Leave, leave, leave, leave now."

What did your model tell you about Katrina?

It showed that most of eastern New Orleans was going to be underwater, with 11 feet of standing water in many places. And it showed there also would be significant flooding just west of the Industrial Canal.

Did you think the model would be accurate?

Yes. We have a lot of faith in our models; we've been working on these models since 2001. We've done a lot of ground-truthing, with storms such as Ivan and Dennis, comparing the actual surge to what we produce.

So you knew that there would be widespread flooding?

We knew that, and we also did some runs where we moved the track west of New Orleans, because that is the absolute worst-case scenario. And so, we knew that if the storm had come west of New Orleans, we were going to flood the whole city.

> 'I think that there is a real lack of appreciation [at FEMA] for the science.'

Obviously, we communicated our findings to everybody we could. Our e-mails go out to a lot of different agencies, but most importantly all the information is sent to the Louisiana Emergency Operations Center, and then everybody who is there is briefed, and that includes senior state officials, Corps of Engineers, military, and so on. By about 10 or 11 PM on Saturday night, everybody over there had been briefed.

Was it a case of your warnings falling on deaf ears?

Well, let me start with the positives. Saturday evening, as soon as we put out our model, the Centers for Disease Control [and Prevention] in Atlanta contacted us and asked if we could do a conference call with them the next morning. So Sunday morning at about 11 AM, we went over all the different potential scenarios with them in terms of flooding, how many people are going to be rescued, what diseases we expect, and so on.

And certainly, we believe the state was aware of what the consequences were going to be. The state has quite a lot of confidence in our modelling, because it's proved accurate in the past. So I think they really recognized that this was going to be serious.

But in terms of the response, it doesn't seem that that urgency—the direness of the situation—got to those in command of, say, FEMA [Federal Emergency Management Agency].

Broken Promises

Do you think FEMA officials and others were reluctant to believe the science, believe the models?

I think that there is a real lack of appreciation for the science. I know from the exercises we've been involved in, certainly with FEMA officials, not all of them have been very responsive. You know, I think a lot of them are ex-military folk, and to them we may be geeks.

So at the Hurricane Pam exercise you did with FEMA in July of 2004, to play out a scenario of a major disaster, not all of the officials took what you had to say seriously?

At the Hurricane Pam exercise we had a number of officials who basically scoffed at us when we were talking about the potential of levees going and the very real threat to New Orleans of a major hurricane. I think they just believed it wouldn't happen.

There were other officials who did. Certainly at Jefferson Parish, they really paid heed to what we had to say, and we did a lot of work with them in helping them to understand.

The other important thing about the Pam exercise is that a lot of local officials came away from it understanding that FEMA, the Federal Emergency Management Agency, had to act within 48 hours—that FEMA would arrive with all the troops, all the food, all the water, and all the rescuers that we needed.

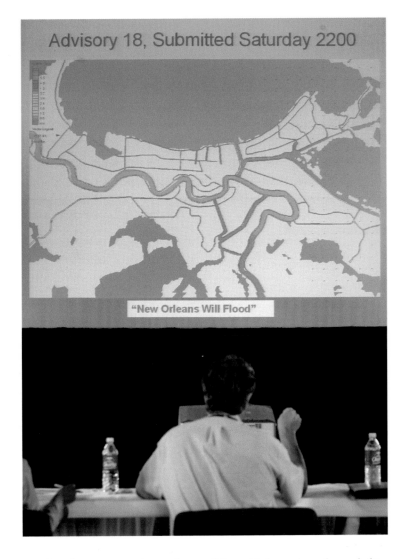

Ivor van Heerden, then director of the Louisiana State University Hurricane Center, makes a presentation to the US Congress about the levees in Southern Louisiana in July 2006. (© AP Images/ Bill Haber.)

You've been warning about New Orleans' vulnerability to a big storm for years. If more government officials had heeded such warnings earlier on, could things have played out differently?

Yes. There were so many different areas where we could have seen a much better response from the government. Number one, we could have had the evacuation of the 57,000 families in New Orleans who don't own motor vehicles completed before the storm arrived. That's the first thing.

The second thing is, we could have had military transport aircraft flying into the New Orleans Airport—it was serviceable early on Tuesday [August 30]—bringing food and water, the necessary amphibious vehicles if needed. There was a promise that in 48 hours, FEMA would start delivering all those things. You know, we look at the Iraq War, and one of the first things our military did was to try and secure the Baghdad Airport, to use it as a staging base. The federal government could have done that in New Orleans. It didn't. So that's why we had this absolutely agonizing situation of the evacuation taking until almost five days later.

> 'I think all of us had been lulled into a sense of security by the continual assurance . . . that the levees were never going to fail.'

Also, desperate people do desperate things. We had violence developing in the city, and the feds again didn't move fast enough to bring in the resources to back up the [people and agencies here] who were trying to keep control. So that's another failure.

But the failing that is the absolute most damning of all was the Corps [of Engineers] should have been monitoring the levees, and they should have warned everybody when they let go. People went to bed on Monday evening—houses dry—and woke up in the middle of the night with water up to their waists. Those are the people that were forced up into their attics, many of them old and frail, because those are the ones who couldn't evacuate. And they didn't have the power to kick out their roofs, or couldn't get an axe or a chainsaw to do so.

The biggest failing in all of this was we should have warned everybody. We could have told the media on Monday night. The levees apparently broke Monday afternoon—the ones that really flooded the main city of New Orleans. We could have got to the media. We could have had vehicles driving on the interstates with bull-horns, telling people. We even could have used helicopters with bullhorns. We could have warned the people, "A big flood's coming, take evasive action." We didn't.

Catastrophic Failure

Did you expect the levee failures?

You know, I think all of us had been lulled into a sense of security by the continual assurance by the Corps of Engineers that the levees were never going to fail. Obviously, this was not the case.

Before Katrina arrived I had looked at just about every single levee in the Greater New Orleans area, and I definitely had some concerns about some of the designs. The Louisiana soils, when they get waterlogged, get very, very soft, and I was worried that some of the earthen levees might not stand the pressure.

How many breaches were there in the various levees?

There were 28 different breaches.

Can you just describe the two main ones?

The 17th Street canal breach was over 600 feet long. The London Avenue canal had two breaches, both about 300–400 feet long. The field evidence shows that there was catastrophic structural failure of these levees. Basically, the whole levee system, including part of the dyke, slid sideways, in some cases almost 30 feet due to the pressure of the water.

Why did the levees collapse?

Well, a lot of that's still under investigation, but the preliminary suggestions are that a) the foundations weren't

Flaws in the New Orleans Levee System

The [New Orleans levee] system did not perform as a system. In some areas it was not completed, and in others, datum misinterpretation and subsidence reduced its intended protective elevation. . . . The capacity for protection varied because of some structures that provided no reliable protection above their design elevations and others that had inadequate designs, leaving them vulnerable at water elevations significantly below the design intent. . . . Katrina created record surge and wave conditions along the east side of New Orleans and the coast of Mississippi. Peak water levels along the Plaquemines and St. Bernard levees and within the Inner Harbor Navigation Canal (IHNC) were significantly higher than the structures, leading to massive overtopping and eventually breaching. . . . Hurricane Katrina resulted in 50 major breaches. With the exception of four levee-flood wall foundation design failures, all of the major breaches (a total of 46) were caused by overtopping and subsequent erosion. Protective elevations that were below those required by the design caused an increase in the amount of overtopping, erosion, and subsequent flooding, particularly in Orleans East. Ironically, the structures that ultimately breached performed as designed, providing protection until overtopping occurred and then becoming vulnerable to catastrophic breaching. The lack of resilience to overtopping significantly increased flooding and resultant losses. The levee-floodwall designs for the 17th Street and London Avenue Outfall Canals and the IHNC were inadequate. In four cases the structures failed catastrophically prior to water reaching design elevations. A significant number of structures that were subjected to water levels beyond their design limits performed well. Typically, in the case of floodwalls, they represented more conservative design assumptions and, for levees, use of higher quality, less erodible materials. The pump stations were largely inoperable during Katrina due to lack of resilience in their power supplies and safe havens for operators.

SOURCE. *US Army Corps of Engineers,* Performance Evaluation of the New Orleans and Southeast Louisiana Hurricane Protection System: Final Report of the Interagency Performance Evaluation Task Force, *vol. 1, June 2009, pp. I-2–I-3. http://biotech.law .lsu.edu/katrina/ipet/Volume%20I%20 FINAL%2023Jun09%20mh.pdf.*

deep enough and b) there might have been some design and construction problems and that [the levees] were weaker than they should have been.

The Corps of Engineers says that the levees were designed to withstand a Category 3 storm. Wasn't Katrina just too strong for them?

Hurricane Katrina was a weak 4 and it may have only been a Category 3. But the London Avenue and 17th Street canals did not experience Category 3 conditions. They experienced conditions of a Category 1 or Category 2 storm, because they were on the left-hand side of the eye—the side that gets the least surge and the least wind.

So the design criteria weren't exceeded. What is now very obvious is that these walls were underengineered. And as a consequence, there was a catastrophic structural failure.

Whose fault is it?

Those levees were designed and owned and maintained by the U.S. Army Corps of Engineers. They chose and supervised and inspected the contractors who built them, so the failure is the responsibility of the U.S. Army Corps of Engineers.

Could floodgates have helped prevent the collapse?

Floodgates could certainly have stopped the surge from moving up those canals. The weak link on those two particular canals, the 17th Street and London Avenue, was the fact that they were open to the lake. We could have put barriers across the mouths of these canals. They would have been very easy to design and construct, and that is part of the catastrophe of New Orleans, that they weren't there.

Aiding the Rescue and Preparing for the Future

As the city flooded, what were you and your team doing?

As soon as Katrina had passed through I contacted our funding agency and asked if I could divert our research funds to operational support. So we immediately got a mapping group organized at the Emergency Operations Center. They started producing maps for search and rescue, mapping the 911 emergency calls, producing other flood-related maps. We had other crews immediately going out to assess the level of damage so that rescuers could understand which areas they needed to concentrate on. And obviously we had a role with the state in advising them of what the next aspect of this disaster was going to be.

And what now?

We're trying to characterize what happened in Katrina. What worked, what didn't work? How good were our models, and how can we modify our models for the future? We want to make all this available so that others will be able to use that information to better understand what the impacts could be if a major hurricane hit their area. This can help a lot of different governmental agencies both here and overseas in designing the structures and infrastructure for coastal cities, so that these governmental agencies, no matter where they are in the world, will be better prepared.

You know, we would hate to see the tragedy of Katrina repeated anywhere else in the world. Here, literally, government didn't come to the aid of the people. Now that we've seen it, now that we know the real outcomes, now that we've got the science to back it up, hopefully others will learn from the mistakes that were committed during Katrina.

How should New Orleans be rebuilt? And do you think that New Orleans will ever be the same again?

Hopefully the federal government gets one thing right, and that is to rebuild Louisiana the way it should be done. We need to come up with a very secure hurricane protection system. We need to rebuild those coastal wetlands so we can get the full benefits in terms of surge reduction. We need to run all of those activities through the city of New Orleans so we regenerate the New Orleans economy.

And hopefully New Orleans will recover. It's never going to be the same again. One hundred thousand people lost everything: they lost their homes. Many, many of those families didn't have any flood insurance, so they're penniless, without a job. And they are spread all over the United States.

> 'The federal government's involvement in Katrina was disgustingly slow.'

Unless the federal government admits its blame in that the levees that it built weren't up to the task and compensates all those people, those folk are never going to come back, and the longer it takes to get them compensation and to get the city cleaned up, the less chance there is of any of those residents ever returning.

Disgust and Heartache

It's clear you are upset about how the federal government responded to Katrina.

The federal government's involvement in Katrina was disgustingly slow. It was unbelievable, especially because we'd done the Hurricane Pam exercise and I had even briefed White House officials.

And, you know, for me, I grew up in apartheid South Africa, and what I saw in a lot of the images was mostly white policemen and military officials ordering mostly black Americans around. And I flashed back on the apartheid scenes that I saw back in the 1980s. It was totally disgusting, and the federal government really needs to apologize to every one of those people.

It's been five weeks since Katrina. How does it make you feel to see the city now—with vast amounts of it still unoccupied, and some areas looking like they won't ever be occupied again?

I was in New Orleans again yesterday all day, and I went into some areas I hadn't been before where the devastation was even worse than I had seen previously. You know, I'm really, really heartsore for those people. Every home has a story. Every home had a life. Every home had a family.

And you walk past some of these homes—only half of them are standing, because they've been destroyed by the floods—and you see on the mantelpiece photographs, family photographs. You walk down the road and you see little trophies that kids got for playing soccer, you know.

They've lost so much, so, so much. And I think that's the really hard part for me to take—as I knew it was coming. And to go and see it day after day is really distressing, and I really hope the federal government admits its wrongs and compensates those people, because they deserve it.

The Government Was Unprepared for Hurricane Katrina

United States Senate

In the following viewpoint, the US Senate presents a report on the government's response to Hurricane Katrina. The Committee on Homeland Security and Government Affairs finds that the impact of the natural disaster was worsened by the failure to prepare for the storm at federal, state, and local levels. The authors highlight the major government failings prior to the storm as well as the use of ineffective response systems after the hurricane made landfall. The committee offers recommendations for a new national emergency-management system in order for the nation to be better prepared for natural catastrophes in the future.

SOURCE. United States Senate, *Hurricane Katrina: A Nation Still Unprepared*, Special Report of the Committee on Homeland Security and Governmental Affairs, S. Rept. No. 109-322. Washington, DC: Government Printing Office, 2006. www.gpo.gov. Public Domain.

Hurricane Katrina was an extraordinary act of nature that spawned a human tragedy. It was the most destructive natural disaster in American history, laying waste to 90,000 square miles of land, an area the size of the United Kingdom. In Mississippi, the storm surge obliterated coastal communities and left thousands destitute. New Orleans was overwhelmed by flooding. All told, more than 1,500 people died. Along the Gulf Coast, tens of thousands suffered without basic essentials for almost a week.

> The results [of the government's failures] were tragic loss of life and human suffering on a massive scale.

But the suffering that continued in the days and weeks after the storm passed did not happen in a vacuum; instead, it continued longer than it should have because of—and was in some cases exacerbated by—the failure of government at all levels to plan, prepare for, and respond aggressively to the storm. These failures were not just conspicuous; they were pervasive. Among the many factors that contributed to these failures, the Committee [on Homeland Security and Government Affairs] found that there were four overarching ones:

1. Long-term warnings went unheeded and government officials neglected their duties to prepare for a forewarned catastrophe;

2. Government officials took insufficient actions or made poor decisions in the days immediately before and after landfall;

3. Systems on which officials relied on to support their response efforts failed; and

4. Government officials at all levels failed to provide effective leadership.

These individual failures, moreover, occurred against a backdrop of failure, over time, to develop the capacity for a coordinated, national response to a truly catastrophic event, whether caused by nature or man-made.

The results were tragic loss of life and human suffering on a massive scale, and an undermining of confidence in our governments' ability to plan, prepare for, and respond to national catastrophes. . . .

Long-Term and Short-Term Warnings Went Unheeded

The Committee has worked to identify and understand the sources of the government's inadequate response and recovery efforts. And while this [viewpoint] does not purport to have identified every such source, it is clear that there was no lack of information about the devastating potential of Katrina, or the uncertain strength of the levees and floodwalls protecting New Orleans, or the

Congressman Tom Davis, the chairman of the House Select Hurricane Katrina Committee, arrives at a February 15, 2006, press conference about the committee's report. (© Joshua Roberts/Getty Images.)

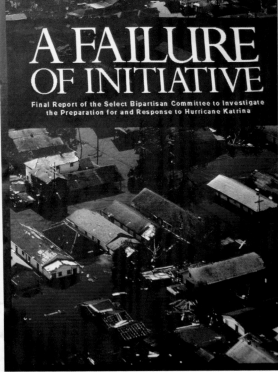

A FAILURE
OF INITIATIVE

Final Report of the Select Bipartisan Committee to Investigate
the Preparation for and Response to Hurricane Katrina

likely needs of survivors. Nonetheless, top officials at every level of government—despite strongly worded advisories from the National Hurricane Center (NHC) and personal warnings from NHC Director Max Mayfield—did not appear to truly grasp the magnitude of the storm's potential for destruction before it made landfall.

The potentially devastating threat of a catastrophic hurricane to the Gulf Coast has been known for 40 years: New Orleans experienced flooding in some areas of remarkably similar proportions from Hurricane Betsy in 1965, and Hurricane Camille devastated the Gulf Coast in 1969. More recently, numerous experts and governmental officials had been anticipating an increase in violent hurricanes, and New Orleans' special and growing vulnerability to catastrophic flooding due to changing geological and other conditions was widely described in both technical and popular media. . . .

Preparation Proved Insufficient

Katrina was not a "typical" hurricane as it approached landfall; it was much larger, more powerful, and was capable of producing catastrophic damage.

In some respects, officials did prepare for Katrina with the understanding that it could be a catastrophe. Some coastal towns in Mississippi went to extraordinary lengths to get citizens to evacuate, including sending people door-to-door to convince and cajole people to move out of harm's way. The State of Louisiana activated more than twice the number of National Guard troops called to duty in any prior hurricane, and achieved the largest evacuation of a threatened population ever to occur. The City of New Orleans issued its first ever mandatory evacuation order. The Coast Guard readied its personnel, pre-positioned its equipment, and stood by to begin search-and-rescue operations as quickly as humanly possible. Departing from usual practice, the governors of the three affected states requested, and

President [George W.] Bush issued, emergency declarations before the storm made landfall.

But however vigorous these preparations, ineffective leadership, poor advance planning, and an unwillingness to devote sufficient resources to emergency management over the long term doomed them to fail when Katrina struck. Despite the understanding of the Gulf Coast's particular vulnerability to hurricane devastation, officials braced for Katrina with full awareness of critical deficiencies in their plans and gaping holes in their resources. While Katrina's destructive force could not be denied, state and local officials did not marshal enough of the resources at their disposal. . . .

> Officials braced for Katrina with full awareness of critical deficiencies in their plans and gaping holes in their resources.

The Committee believes that leadership failures needlessly compounded these losses. New Orleans Mayor Ray Nagin and Louisiana Governor Kathleen Blanco—who knew the limitations of their resources to address a catastrophe—did not specify those needs adequately to the federal government before landfall. For example, while Governor Blanco stated in a letter to President Bush, two days before landfall, that she anticipated the resources of the state would be overwhelmed, she made no specific request for assistance in evacuating the known tens of thousands of people without means of transportation, and a senior State official identified no unmet needs in response to a federal offer of assistance the following day. The State's transportation secretary also ignored his responsibilities under the state's emergency operations plan, leaving no arm of the State government prepared to obtain and deliver additional transportation to those in New Orleans who lacked it when Katrina struck. In view of the long-standing role of requests as a trigger for action by higher levels of government, the State bears responsibility for not signaling its needs to the federal government more clearly.

Compounded by leadership failures of its own, the federal government bears responsibility for not preparing effectively for its role in the post-storm response.

FEMA was unprepared for a catastrophic event of the scale of Katrina. Well before Katrina, FEMA's relationships with state and local officials, once a strength, had been eroded in part because certain preparedness grant programs were transferred elsewhere in the Department of Homeland Security (DHS). With its importance to state and local preparedness activities reduced, FEMA's effectiveness was diminished. In addition, at no time in its history, including in the years before it became part of DHS, had FEMA developed—nor had it been designed to develop—response capabilities sufficient for a catastrophe, nor had it developed the capacity to mobilize sufficient resources from other federal agencies, and the private and nonprofit sectors. . . .

In addition, the White House shares responsibility for the inadequate pre-landfall preparations. To be sure, President Bush, at the request of [FEMA's former director Michael] Brown, did take the initiative to personally call Governor Blanco to urge a mandatory evacuation. As noted earlier, he also took the unusual step of declaring an emergency in the Gulf Coast States prior to Katrina's landfall. On the other hand, the President did not leave his Texas ranch to return to Washington until two days after landfall, and only then convened his Cabinet, as well as a White House task force, to oversee federal response efforts.

Response at All Levels of Government Was Unacceptable

The effect of the long-term failures at every level of government to plan and prepare adequately for a catastrophic hurricane in the Gulf of Mexico was evident in the inadequate preparations before Katrina's landfall and then again in the initial response to the storm.

Flooding in New Orleans drove thousands of survivors to attics and rooftops to await rescue. Some people were trapped in attics and nursing homes and drowned as the dirty waters rose around them. Others escaped only by chopping their way through roofs. Infrastructure damage complicated the organization and conduct of search-and-rescue missions in New Orleans and elsewhere. Destruction of communications towers and equipment, in particular, limited the ability of crews to communicate with one another, undermining coordination and efficiency. Rescuers also had to contend with weapons fire, debris, and polluted water. The skill and dedication of Louisiana Department of Wildlife and Fisheries (W&F) officials and others working in these adverse conditions stand out as a singular success story of the hurricane response. . . .

> Infrastructure damage complicated the organization and conduct of search-and-rescue missions.

The City of New Orleans was unprepared to help people evacuate, as many buses from the city's own fleet were submerged, while officials had not arranged in advance for drivers for those buses that were available.

The storm also laid waste to much of the city's police, whose headquarters and several district offices, along with hundreds of vehicles, rounds of ammunition, and uniforms were all destroyed within the first two days of landfall.

Planning for search and rescue was also insufficient. FEMA, for instance, failed to provide boats for its search-and-rescue teams even though flooding had been confirmed by Tuesday [August 30, 2005]. Moreover, interagency coordination was inadequate at both the state and federal levels. . . .

Long-Term Factors Contributed to the Poor Response

Actions taken—and failures to act—well before Katrina struck compounded the problems resulting from the ineffective leadership that characterized the immediate preparations for the hurricane and the post-landfall response. A common theme of these earlier actions is underfunding emergency preparedness. While the Committee did not examine the conflicting political or budget priorities that may have played a role, in many cases the shortsightedness associated with the underfunding is glaring. . . .

The Levee System Was Inadequate

These planning failures would have been of far less consequence had the system of levees built to protect New Orleans from flooding stayed intact, as they had in most prior hurricanes. But they did not, and the resulting inundation was catastrophic. The levee failures themselves turned out to have roots long predating Katrina as well. While several engineering analyses continue, the Committee found deeply disturbing evidence of flaws in the design and construction of the levees. For instance, two major drainage canals—the 17th Street and London Avenue Canals—failed at their foundations, prior to their flood walls being met with the water heights for which they were designed to protect central New Orleans.

> The levee failures themselves turned out to have roots long predating Katrina as well.

Moreover, the greater metropolitan New Orleans area was literally riddled with levee breaches caused by massive overtopping and scouring of levees that were not "armored," or properly designed, to guard against the cascading waters that would inevitably accompany a storm of the magnitude of Hurricane Katrina. The Committee also discovered that the inspection-and-maintenance regime in place to ensure that the levees, floodwalls, and other structures built to protect the residents of the greater New Orleans area was in no way commensurate with the risk posed to these persons and their property.

Equally troubling was the revelation of serious disagreement—still unresolved months after Katrina—among officials of several government entities over who had responsibility, and when, for key levee issues including emergency response and levee repair. Such conflicts prevented any meaningful emergency plans from being put in place and, at the time of Katrina, none of the relevant government agencies had a plan for responding to a levee breach. While the deadly waters continued to pour into the heart of the city after the hurricane had passed, the very government agencies that were supposed to work together to protect the city from such a catastrophe not only initially disagreed about whose responsibility it was to repair the levee breaches, but disagreed as to how the repairs should be conducted. Sadly, due to the lack of foresight and overall coordination prior to the storm, such conflicts existed as the waters of Lake Pontchartrain continued to fill central New Orleans. . . .

Recommendations: A New National Emergency-Management System for the 21st Century

The Committee's Report sets out seven core recommendations together with a series of supporting tactical recommendations, all designed to make the nation's emergency-preparedness and response system strong, agile, effective, and robust.

Hurricane Katrina exposed flaws in the structure of FEMA and DHS that are too substantial to mend. *Our first core recommendation is to abolish FEMA and replace it with a stronger, more capable structure, to be known* as the National Preparedness and Response Authority (NPRA). . . .

Our second core recommendation is to endow the new organization with the full range of responsibilities that are core to preparing for and responding to disasters. These include the four central functions of comprehensive emergency management—mitigation, preparedness, response, and recovery—which need to be integrated. . . .

Our third core recommendation is to enhance regional operations to provide better coordination between federal agencies and the states and establish regional strike teams. Regional offices should be adequately staffed, with representation from federal agencies outside DHS that are likely to be called on to respond to a significant disaster in the region. They should provide coordination and assist in planning, training, and exercising of emergency-preparedness and response activities; work with states to ensure that grant funds are spent most effectively; coordinate and develop inter-state agreements; enhance coordination with non-governmental organizations and the private sector; and provide personnel and assets, in the form of Strike Teams, to be the federal government's first line of response to a disaster. . . .

> The Committee shares the view expressed by President Bush . . . that our nation can do better.

Our fourth core recommendation is to build a true, government-wide operations center to provide enhanced situational awareness and manage interagency coordination in a disaster. . . .

Our fifth core recommendation is to renew and sustain commitments at all levels of government to the nation's emergency core management system. FEMA emergency-response teams have been reduced substantially in size, are inadequately equipped, and training for these teams has been all but eliminated. If the federal government is to improve its performance and be prepared to respond effectively to the next disaster, we must give NPRA—and the other federal agencies with central responsibilities under the NRP [National Response Plan]—the necessary resources to accomplish this. . . .

Our sixth core recommendation is to strengthen the underpinning of the nation's response to disasters and catastrophes. Despite their shortcomings and imperfections, the NRP and National Incident Management System (NIMS), including the Emergency Support Function (ESF) structure currently represent the best approach available to respond to multi-agency, multi-jurisdictional emergencies. Federal, state, and local officials and other responders must commit to supporting the NRP and NIMS and working together to improve the performance of the national emergency management system. . . .

Our seventh core recommendation is to improve the nation's capacity to respond to catastrophic events. DHS should ensure that the Catastrophic Incident Annex (CIA) is fully understood by the federal departments and agencies with responsibilities associated with it. The Catastrophic Incident Supplement (CIS) should be completed and published, and the supporting operational plans for departments and agencies with responsibilities under the CIA should be completed. These plans should be reviewed and coordinated with the states, and on a regional basis, to ensure they are understood, trained and exercised prior to an emergency. . . .

The United States Must Be Prepared for Catastrophes

The Committee's Report can do justice neither to the human suffering endured during and after Katrina nor to the dimensions of the response. As to the latter, we have identified many successes and many failures; no doubt there are others in both categories we have missed. The Committee shares the view expressed by President Bush shortly after Katrina that our nation can do better.

Avoiding past mistakes will not suffice. Our leadership and systems must be prepared for catastrophes we know will be unlike Katrina, whether due to natural causes or terrorism. The Committee hopes to help meet that goal through the recommendations in this Report, because almost exactly four years after [the al Qaeda–coordinated terrorist attacks of] 9/11, Katrina showed that the nation is still unprepared.

The Government Learned Many Lessons from Hurricane Katrina Failures

George W. Bush Administration

In the following viewpoint, the administration of former president George W. Bush reviews the federal government's response to Hurricane Katrina. The administration examines the challenges that the hurricane presented, as well as failings in the government's response to each challenge. The viewpoint highlights the key lessons that the federal government has learned from the aftermath of the storm. The purpose of this examination, the administration states, is to improve the nation's preparedness for natural disasters in the future. George W. Bush was the forty-third president of the United States, from 2001 to 2009.

SOURCE. George W. Bush Administration, "Chapter 5: Lessons Learned," *The Federal Response to Hurricane Katrina: Lessons Learned*, The White House, February 2006. http://georgewbush-whitehouse .archives.gov. Public Domain.

While there were numerous stories of great professionalism, courage, and compassion by Americans from all walks of life, our task here is to identify the critical challenges that undermined and prevented a more efficient and effective Federal response. In short, what were the key failures during the Federal response to Hurricane Katrina?

We ask this question not to affix blame. Rather, we endeavor to find the answers in order to identify systemic gaps and improve our preparedness for the next disaster—natural or man-made. We must move promptly to understand precisely what went wrong and determine how we are going to fix it. . . .

> The Department of Defense . . . has the capability to play a critical role in the Nation's response to catastrophic events.

Critical Challenge: National Preparedness

Our current system for homeland security does not provide the necessary framework to manage the challenges posed by 21st Century catastrophic threats. But to be clear, it is unrealistic to think that even the strongest framework can perfectly anticipate and overcome all challenges in a crisis. While we have built a response system that ably handles the demands of a typical hurricane season, wildfires, and other limited natural and man-made disasters, the system clearly has structural flaws for addressing catastrophic events. During the Federal response to Katrina, four critical flaws in our national preparedness became evident: Our processes for unified management of the national response; command and control structures within the Federal government; knowledge of our preparedness plans; and regional planning and coordination. . . .

Lessons Learned: The Federal government should work with its homeland security partners in revising existing plans, ensuring a functional operational structure—including within regions—and establishing a clear, accountable process for all National preparedness efforts. In doing so, the Federal government must:

- Ensure that Executive Branch agencies are organized, trained, and equipped to perform their response roles.

- Finalize and implement the National Preparedness Goal.

Critical Challenge: Integrated Use of Military Capabilities

The Federal response to Hurricane Katrina demonstrates that the Department of Defense (DOD) has the capability to play a critical role in the Nation's response to catastrophic events. During the Katrina response, DOD—both National Guard and active duty forces—demonstrated that along with the Coast Guard it was one of the only Federal departments that possessed real operational capabilities to translate Presidential decisions into prompt, effective action on the ground. . . . Yet DOD capabilities must be better identified and integrated into the Nation's response plans. . . .

> The Federal government must be prepared to fulfill the mission if State and local efforts fail.

Lessons Learned: The Departments of Homeland Security and Defense should jointly plan for the Department of Defense's support of Federal response activities as well as those extraordinary circumstances when it is appropriate for the Department of Defense to lead the Federal response. In addition, the Department of Defense should ensure the transformation of the National Guard is focused on increased integration with active duty forces for homeland security plans and activities.

Critical Challenge: Communications

Hurricane Katrina destroyed an unprecedented portion of the core communications infrastructure throughout the Gulf Coast region. As described earlier in the Report, the storm debilitated 911 emergency call centers, disrupting local emergency services. Nearly three million customers lost telephone service. Broadcast communications, including 50 percent of area radio stations and 44 percent of area television stations, similarly were affected. More than 50,000 utility poles were toppled in Mississippi alone, meaning that even if telephone call centers and electricity generation capabilities were functioning, the connections to the customers were broken. . . .

Lessons Learned: The Department of Homeland Security should review our current laws, policies, plans, and strategies relevant to communications. Upon the conclusion of this review, the Homeland Security Council, with support from the Office of Science and Technology Policy, should develop a National Emergency Communications Strategy that supports communications operability and interoperability. . . .

Critical Challenge: Logistics and Evacuation

Throughout the response, Federal resource managers had great difficulty determining what resources were needed, what resources were available, and where those resources were at any given point in time. Even when Federal resource managers had a clear understanding of what was needed, they often could not readily determine whether the Federal government had that asset, or what alternative sources might be able to provide it. . . . FEMA's [Federal Emergency Management Agency] lack of a real-time asset-tracking system—a necessity for successful 21st Century businesses—left Federal managers in the dark regarding the status of resources once they were shipped. . . .

Lessons Learned: The Department of Homeland Security, in coordination with State and local governments and the private sector, should develop a modern, flexible, and transparent logistics system. This system should be based on established contracts for stockpiling commodities at the local level for emergencies and the provision of goods and services during emergencies. The Federal government must develop the capacity to conduct large-scale logistical operations that supplement and, if necessary, replace State and local logistical systems by leveraging resources within both the public sector and the private sector.

With respect to evacuation . . . the Hurricane Katrina experience demonstrates that the Federal government must be prepared to fulfill the mission if State and local efforts fail. Unfortunately, a lack of prior planning combined with poor operational coordination generated a weak Federal performance in supporting the evacuation of those most vulnerable in New Orleans and throughout the Gulf Coast following Katrina's landfall. The Federal effort lacked critical elements of prior planning, such as evacuation routes, communications, transportation assets, evacuee processing, and coordination with State, local, and non-governmental officials receiving and sheltering the evacuees. . . . FEMA also had difficulty delivering food, water, and other critical commodities to people waiting to be evacuated, most significantly at the Superdome.

Lessons Learned: The Department of Transportation, in coordination with other appropriate departments of the Executive Branch, must also be prepared to conduct mass evacuation operations when disasters overwhelm or incapacitate State and local governments.

Critical Challenge: Search and Rescue

After Hurricane Katrina made landfall, rising floodwaters stranded thousands in New Orleans on rooftops, requiring a massive civil search and rescue operation. The Coast Guard, FEMA Urban Search and Rescue (US&R) Task Forces, and DOD forces, in concert with State and local emergency responders from across the country, courageously combined to rescue tens of thousands of people. With extraordinary ingenuity and tenacity, Federal, State, and local emergency responders plucked people from rooftops while avoiding urban hazards not normally encountered during waterborne rescue.

Yet many of these courageous lifesavers were put at unnecessary risk by a structure that failed to support them effectively. . . .

Lessons Learned: The Department of Homeland Security should lead an interagency review of current policies and procedures to ensure effective integration of all Federal search and rescue assets during disaster response.

Critical Challenge: Public Safety and Security

State and local governments have a fundamental responsibility to provide for the public safety and security of their residents. During disasters, the Federal government provides law enforcement assistance only when those resources are overwhelmed or depleted. Almost immediately following Hurricane Katrina's landfall, law and order began to deteriorate in New Orleans. The city's overwhelmed police force—70 percent of which were themselves victims of the disaster—did not have the capacity to arrest every person witnessed committing a crime, and many more crimes were undoubtedly neither observed by police nor reported. The resulting lawlessness in New Orleans significantly impeded—and in some cases temporarily halted—relief efforts and delayed restoration of essential private sector services such as power, water, and telecommunications. . . .

Lessons Learned: The Department of Justice, in coordination with the Department of Homeland Security, should examine Federal responsibilities for support to State and local law enforcement and criminal justice systems during emergencies and then build operational plans, procedures, and policies to ensure an effective Federal law enforcement response.

Critical Challenge: Public Health and Medical Support

Hurricane Katrina created enormous public health and medical challenges, especially in Louisiana and Mississippi—States with public health infrastructures that ranked 49th and 50th in the Nation, respectively. But it was the subsequent flooding of New Orleans that imposed catastrophic public health conditions on the people of southern Louisiana and forced an unprecedented mobilization of Federal public health and medical assets. Tens of thousands of people required medical care. Over 200,000 people with chronic medical conditions, displaced by the storm and isolated by the flooding, found themselves without access to their usual medications and sources of medical care. Several large hospitals were totally destroyed and many others were rendered inoperable. Nearly all smaller health care facilities were shut down. Although public health and medical support efforts restored the capabilities of many of these facilities, the region's health care infrastructure sustained extraordinary damage.

> Most local and State public health and medical assets were overwhelmed.

Most local and State public health and medical assets were overwhelmed by these conditions. . . .

Rescue crews search neighborhoods of New Orleans as floodwaters recede on September 14, 2005, in the aftermath of Hurricane Katrina. (© Chris Graythen/Getty Images.)

Lessons Learned: In coordination with the Department of Homeland Security and other homeland security partners, the Department of Health and Human Services should strengthen the Federal government's capability to provide public health and medical support during a crisis. This will require the improvement of command and control of public health resources, the development of deliberate plans, an additional investment in deployable operational resources, and an acceleration of the initiative to foster the widespread use of interoperable electronic health records systems.

Critical Challenge: Human Services

Disasters—especially those of catastrophic proportions —produce many victims whose needs exceed the capacity of State and local resources. These victims who depend on the Federal government for assistance fit into one of two categories: (1) those who need Federal disaster-related assistance, and (2) those who need continuation of government assistance they were receiving before the disaster, plus additional disaster-related assistance. Hurricane Katrina produced many thousands of both categories of victims. . . .

Lessons Learned: The Department of Health and Human Services should coordinate with other departments of the Executive Branch, as well as State governments and non-governmental organizations, to develop a robust, comprehensive, and integrated system to deliver human services during disasters so that victims are able to receive Federal and State assistance in a simple and seamless manner. In particular, this system should be designed to provide victims a consumer oriented, simple, effective, and single encounter from which they can receive assistance.

Critical Challenge: Mass Care and Housing

Hurricane Katrina resulted in the largest national housing crisis since the Dust Bowl of the 1930s. The impact of this massive displacement was felt throughout the country, with Gulf residents relocating to all fifty States and the District of Columbia. Prior to the storm's landfall, an exodus of people fled its projected path, creating an urgent need for suitable shelters. Those with the willingness and ability to evacuate generally found temporary shelter or housing. However, the thousands of people in New Orleans who were either unable to move due to health reasons or lack of transportation, or who simply did not choose to comply with the mandatory evacuation order, had significant difficulty finding suitable shelter after the hurricane had devastated the city.

Overall, Federal, State, and local plans were inadequate for a catastrophe that had been anticipated for years. . . .

Lessons Learned: Using established Federal core competencies and all available resources, the Department of

Housing and Urban Development, in coordination with other departments of the Executive Branch with housing stock, should develop integrated plans and bolstered capabilities for the temporary and long-term housing of evacuees. The American Red Cross and the Department of Homeland Security should retain responsibility and improve the process of mass care and sheltering during disasters.

> "We can be certain that their [the NOAA's] efforts saved lives."

Critical Challenge: Public Communications

The Federal government's dissemination of essential public information prior to Hurricane Katrina's Gulf landfall is one of the positive lessons learned. The many professionals at the National Oceanic and Atmospheric Administration (NOAA) and the National Hurricane Center worked with diligence and determination in disseminating weather reports and hurricane track predictions. . . . We can be certain that their efforts saved lives.

However, more could have been done by officials at all levels of government. . . .

Lessons Learned: The Department of Homeland Security should develop an integrated public communications plan to better inform, guide, and reassure the American public before, during, and after a catastrophe. The Department of Homeland Security should enable this plan with operational capabilities to deploy coordinated public affairs teams during a crisis.

Critical Challenge: Critical Infrastructure and Impact Assessment

Hurricane Katrina had a significant impact on many sectors of the region's "critical infrastructure," especially the energy sector. The Hurricane temporarily caused the shutdown of most crude oil and natural gas production in the Gulf of Mexico as well as much of the refining capacity in Louisiana, Mississippi, and Alabama. . . . Across the region more than 2.5 million customers suffered power outages across Louisiana, Mississippi, and Alabama. . . .

Lessons Learned: The Department of Homeland Security, working collaboratively with the private sector, should revise the National Response Plan and finalize the Interim National Infrastructure Protection Plan to be able to rapidly assess the impact of a disaster on critical infrastructure. We must use this knowledge to inform Federal response and prioritization decisions and to support infrastructure restoration in order to save lives and mitigate the impact of the disaster on the Nation.

Critical Challenge: Environmental Hazards and Debris Removal

The Federal clean-up effort for Hurricane Katrina was an immense undertaking. The storm impact caused the spill of over seven million gallons of oil into Gulf Coast waterways. Additionally, it flooded three Superfund sites in the New Orleans area, and destroyed or compromised numerous drinking water facilities and wastewater treatment plants along the Gulf Coast. The storm's collective environmental damage, while not creating the "toxic soup" portrayed in the media, nonetheless did create a potentially hazardous environment for emergency responders and the general public. In response, the Environmental Protection Agency (EPA) and the Coast Guard jointly led an interagency environmental assessment and recovery effort, cleaning up the seven million

> Federal officials could have improved the identification of environmental hazards and communication of appropriate warnings.

gallons of oil and resolving over 2,300 reported cases of pollution.

While this response effort was commendable, Federal officials could have improved the identification of environmental hazards and communication of appropriate warnings to emergency responders and the public. . . .

Lessons Learned: The Department of Homeland Security, in coordination with the Environmental Protection Agency, should oversee efforts to improve the Federal government's capability to quickly gather environmental data and to provide the public and emergency responders the most accurate information available, to determine whether it is safe to operate in a disaster environment or to return after evacuation. In addition, the Department of Homeland Security should work with its State and local homeland security partners to plan and to coordinate an integrated approach to debris removal during and after a disaster.

Critical Challenge: Managing Offers of Foreign Assistance and Inquiries Regarding Affected Foreign Nationals

Our experience with the tragedies of [the al Qaeda–coordinated terrorist attacks of] September 11th [2001] and Hurricane Katrina underscored that our domestic crises have international implications. Soon after the extent of Hurricane Katrina's damage became known, the United States became the beneficiary of an incredible international outpouring of assistance. One hundred fifty-one (151) nations and international organizations offered financial or material assistance to support relief efforts. Also, we found that among the victims were foreign nationals who were in the country on business, vacation, or as residents. Not surprisingly, foreign governments sought information regarding the safety of their citizens.

We were not prepared to make the best use of foreign support. . . .

Lessons Learned: The Department of State, in coordination with the Department of Homeland Security, should review and revise policies, plans, and procedures for the management of foreign disaster assistance. In addition, this review should clarify responsibilities and procedures for handling inquiries regarding affected foreign nationals.

Critical Challenge: Non-governmental Aid

Over the course of the Hurricane Katrina response, a significant capability for response resided in organizations outside of the government. Non-governmental and faith-based organizations [NGOs], as well as the private sector all made substantial contributions. Unfortunately, the Nation did not always make effective use of these contributions because we had not effectively planned for integrating them into the overall response effort. . . .

> NGOs successfully contributed to the relief effort in spite of government obstacles.

More often than not, NGOs successfully contributed to the relief effort in spite of government obstacles and with almost no government support or direction. Time and again, government agencies did not effectively coordinate relief operations with NGOs. Often, government agencies failed to match relief needs with NGO and private sector capabilities. Even when agencies matched non-governmental aid with an identified need, there were problems moving goods, equipment, and people into the disaster area. For example, the government relief effort was unprepared to meet the fundamental food, housing, and operational needs of the surge volunteer force.

Lessons Learned: The Federal response should better integrate the contributions of volunteers and nongovernmental organizations into the broader national effort. This integration would be best achieved at the State and local levels, prior to future incidents. In particular, State and local governments must engage NGOs in the planning process, credential their personnel, and provide them the necessary resource support for their involvement in a joint response.

Americans Felt Shame and Outrage About the Response to Hurricane Katrina

Larry Eichel

In the following viewpoint, a journalist contends that the American people were ashamed and angry at the government's inadequate response to Hurricane Katrina. There is a sense of failure across the nation, the author asserts, and many believe that the United States should have done better in responding to the disaster. He highlights several disastrous outcomes of the storm that were manmade, such as the gap in communication between local and federal government and the lack of a coordinated relief effort. Larry Eichel is a senior writer for the *Philadelphia Inquirer*.

I n the aftermath of [the al Qaeda–coordinated terrorist attacks of] Sept. 11 [2001], most Americans felt a mixture of anger, sorrow and pride.

Anger at the perpetrators. Sorrow from the unthinkable loss. Pride at the brave response.

Oh, how different is Katrina.

The Government's Response to Katrina Is Embarrassing

This past week [August 28–September 2, 2005], there was embarrassment at the sight of people dying of neglect in the streets of New Orleans.

Shame at the violence, the extent of the looting, and the breakdown of societal norms.

And disappointment, even outrage, at the slow and seemingly inadequate response of government from the top down.

Hanging over the still-unfolding catastrophe is an overarching sense of failure, a feeling that the United States in the 21st century ought to have done better—even in dealing with what appears to be [the] worst natural disaster in at least 100 years.

On Friday [September 2, 2005], as he left Washington for a first-hand look at recovery efforts, President [George W.] Bush acknowledged the obvious.

"The results are not acceptable," he said, pledging "to get the situation under control."

After Sept. 11 [2001], leaders rose to the occasion. New York Mayor Rudolph Giuliani took charge immediately, and Bush, after a few missteps, said exactly what America needed to hear.

> In a time of confusion, when leadership was most needed, no one seemed to be running the show.

No One Was in Charge

That didn't happen in the opening days of the Katrina aftermath. In a time of confusion, when leadership was most needed, no one seemed to be running the show.

Although much heroic work was being done, there were few visible heroes, other than the helicopter pilots and the medical personnel.

PUBLIC OPINION ON THE HURRICANE KATRINA DISASTER	White	Black
Personal reactions		
Have felt depressed	55%	73%
Have felt angry	46%	70%
Have a close friend/relative	22%	43%
To get relief efforts moving		
Bush did all he could	31%	11%
Could have done more	63%	85%
Don't know	6%	4%
Federal government response		
Excellent/good	41%	19%
Only fair/poor	55%	77%
Don't know	4%	4%
State and local government response		
Excellent/good	41%	46%
Only fair/poor	51%	48%
Don't know	8%	6%

Taken from: "Huge Racial Divide over Katrina and Its Consequences," Pew Research Center for People and the Press, September 8, 2005. www.people-press.org.

A sign outside a New Orleans home protests the federal response to Hurricane Katrina in September 2005. (© Omar Torres/ AFP/Getty Images.)

And the talk of all the personnel and material government was throwing at the problem wasn't reflected initially on the ground. The gap between word and deed undercut official credibility, breeding bitterness among those most in need.

Not until Friday, four days after the storm and three days after the flood, did National Guard troops secure the New Orleans Convention Center—source of some of the most chilling tales of violence, death and survival—and bring in food, water and medicine.

For most of the week, public officials, including New Orleans Mayor Ray Nagin, frequently were reduced to sounding like helpless bystanders begging for federal assistance, rather than leaders committed to doing all that was in their own power.

One of the most visible federal officials, Michael Brown, director of the Federal Emergency Management Agency, came dangerously close to blaming the victims. In a series of interviews on Thursday, as relief efforts seemed stalled, he kept raising the question of why more New Orleans residents had failed to heed mandatory evacuation orders before the storm hit.

In retrospect, it seems perfectly understandable why many of the poorest residents of one of the nation's poorest cities weren't able to leave. An estimated 50,000 households in New Orleans don't have cars; no buses were available; and many of the poor with cars didn't have the money for motels.

On Friday, a group of African-American political leaders in Washington alleged that one reason why the federal response had not been faster was because so many of the victims are so poor.

To be sure, some of the week's more disturbing events—including the deaths of the frail elderly and the civil disorder—might have happened even if the response had been faster and more efficient.

The storm was of epic proportions, displacing as many as one million people and killing hundreds, perhaps thousands. Once the levees broke in New Orleans, much of the chaos became inevitable.

A Lack of Planning and Communication

But it was hard to understand why for several days reporters could get to the New Orleans Convention

Center—an obvious gathering spot where thousands of the newly homeless lived in squalor and despair—while relief supplies and personnel couldn't.

Or why major New Orleans hospitals, operating without power or sanitary facilities, couldn't be evacuated sooner.

Or why residents, suffering in the Louisiana Superdome and elsewhere, couldn't be moved out of the city more quickly, even if many roads remained under water.

> Officials also underestimated the need for, and difficulty of, providing a police presence in a city with little food, water or hope.

Or why nearly four years after the attacks of Sept. 11, with billions of new dollars having been invested in emergency services, the overall response wasn't better.

As the weekend began, real progress was being made. But why hadn't it come sooner?

Beyond the questions of leadership, a lack of planning was part of the answer. Even though the prospect of a levee-rupturing hurricane striking New Orleans had been discussed for years, officials seemed utterly unprepared when it happened.

Communication was another problem. Once the cell-phone towers went down, the authorities had as much trouble talking to each other as did ordinary citizens. The lack of information made it difficult to deploy resources, once they were assembled, or to coordinate efforts.

Officials also underestimated the need for, and difficulty of, providing a police presence in a city with little food, water or hope. The looting, a means of survival for some, degenerated into a level of disorder that slowed recovery efforts.

On Wednesday night, as New Orleans drifted out of control, Louisiana Gov. Kathleen Blanco said sadly: "What angers me the most is that, usually, disasters like this bring out the best in everybody. And that's what we expected to see. And now we've got people that it's bringing out the worst in."

The storm brought out less than the best in a lot of people, from the thugs in the streets to officials in Washington.

Members of Congress from both parties already are asking what went wrong and what lessons are to be learned—with a major federal investigation sure to come.

In that sense, Hurricane Katrina is a lot like Sept. 11.

Media Hysteria Caused Inaccurate Reporting During Hurricane Katrina

Brian Thevenot

In the following viewpoint, a journalist examines the myths that were reported in the immediate aftermath of Hurricane Katrina. Many stories of violence were exaggerated, the author finds, and passed along to government officials. This led journalists to spread alarmist reports—many of which proved to be false. In a September 26, 2005, New Orleans *Times-Picayune* article, the author published an article correcting misinformation he reported in the initial days after the storm. He explores the media reaction to his article, and why he chose to prove his early reports wrong. Brian Thevenot covered Hurricane Katrina for the *Times-Picayune* and is currently the deputy business editor at the *Los Angeles Times*.

As I walked briskly through the dimly lit area inside the food service entrance of New Orleans' Ernest N. Morial Convention Center, the thought of pulling back the sheets covering the four stinking, decomposing corpses in front of me seemed wrong, even perverse. Before I'd even thought to ask, one of the two soldiers who escorted me, Arkansas National Guardsman Mikel Brooks, nixed the prospect of looking inside the freezer he and another soldier said contained "30 or 40" bodies.

"I ain't got the stomach for it, even after what I saw in Iraq," he said.

I didn't push it. Now I wish I had, as gruesome as that may seem. The soldiers might have branded me a morbid fiend and run me the hell out of there, but my story in the September 6 [2005] edition of the [New Orleans] *Times-Picayune* would have been right, or at least included a line saying I'd been denied the opportunity to lay eyes on the freezer.

Instead, I quoted Brooks and another soldier, by name, about the freezer's allegedly grim inventory, including the statement that it contained a "7-year-old with her throat cut."

Neither the mass of bodies nor the allegedly expired child would ever be found. As I later reported, an internal review by Arkansas Guard Lt. Col. John Edwards found that Brooks and others who repeated the freezer story had heard it in the food line at Harrah's Casino, a law enforcement and military staging area a block away. Edwards told me no soldier had actually seen bodies in a freezer.

I retell this story not to deflect blame—factual errors under my byline are mine alone—but as an example of how one of hundreds of myths got reported in the early days of Hurricane Katrina's aftermath. I corrected the freezer report—along with a slew of other rumors and myths transmitted by the media—in a September 26

Times-Picayune story coauthored by my colleague Gordon Russell. In that piece, we sought to separate fact from fiction on the narrow issue of reported violence at the Louisiana Superdome and the Convention Center.

Debunking Media Myths

We hadn't anticipated the massive shockwave of self-correction that story would send through the international media. The examination of myths of violence—and their confirmation by New Orleans Mayor C. Ray Nagin and then–Police Superintendent Eddie Compass—became the story for days on end, a moment of mass-scale media introspection that ultimately resulted in a healthy revision of history's first draft.

> While anarchy indeed reigned in the city . . . many if not most of the alarmist reports of violence were false.

The *Los Angeles Times*, the *New York Times* and the *Washington Post* followed up with similar, well-researched efforts debunking myths and coming to essentially the same conclusion we had: While anarchy indeed reigned in the city, and subhuman conditions in the Dome and the Convention Center shocked the nation's conscience, many if not most of the alarmist reports of violence were false, or at least could not be verified. Dozens of other newspapers and television outlets joined in, offering news and opinion pieces, many doggedly questioning what they and others had earlier reported.

Our myth-debunking story put me in the eye of the debate's swirling storm. National television outlets praised our work, quoted it frequently and sought me out for interviews as their latest instant expert. A few bloggers had the opposite reaction, hanging me in virtual effigy as a symbol of the failings of the dreaded "MSM"—the mainstream media, that evil monolith—and concocting conspiracy theories to explain the media's errant early reports. Questions of race and class pervaded the debate in all media: Did the reporting of violence stem from journalists' willingness to believe the worst about poor African Americans? What role did the refugees themselves, along with local black public officials—both of whom served as sources for many of the false stories—play in creating the myths?

The *New York Times* tempered its assessment of false reports, writing "some, though not all, of the most alarming stories that coursed through the city appear to be little more than figments of frightened imaginations." But the *Times'* piece differed in scope from ours, assessing reports of crime citywide instead of only at the Dome and the Convention Center. The *Times* also reported on property crimes such as widespread looting—definitely not a myth, I can confirm as an eyewitness—as part of the paper's exhaustive review. We concentrated exclusively on violent crime. . . .

By the time the *Times-Picayune's* story ran—followed quickly by the *L.A. Times'* and the *New York Times'* pieces—nearly a month after the storm, there was no shortage of reports to second-guess. Many were attributed to refugees, cops and soldiers and even top public officials. Others appeared with weak attribution or none at all. . . .

Transitioning from Reporter to Source

Immediately after our story broke, we found ourselves making the rather jarring transition from reporter to source. The cable networks—CNN, MSNBC and Fox—needed to act immediately. It had taken me and Russell a full week to research our piece. So they sought members of our rag-tag "New Orleans bureau" for interviews.

The day the story ran, I went on CNN's "NewsNight with Aaron Brown." . . . "We often remind you, when reporting breaking news stories, that the first reports are often wrong," Brown started. "With Katrina, it turns out that some of those reports, and not just the early ones, were really wrong. Some were fueled by people who were tired and hungry and clearly desperate. But some were fueled by the people in charge."

Knowing I had little time to make a point, I made sure to shift some focus away from the criticism of Nagin and Compass and turn the attention forward, toward correcting the record rather than finger-pointing.

"I have some sympathy for their initial reporting of supposed atrocities at the Dome and the Convention Center," I said of the city leaders. "Their communication apparatus had completely broken down. . . . I also think that the media, in some sense, has to take responsibility for this and to come back to check, to verify some of these stories, basically just to finish the job, as I think we tried to do today."

Brown took the point and moved the conversation toward explaining how confusion created misinformation. "It sounds like there was almost a giant game of post office being played," he said. "One person believes to have seen one thing, tells someone else, and as it goes down the line, it keeps getting bigger and bigger and bigger. Before you know it, you have hundreds of deaths."

I concurred. "There was a quote in the story today, I think a smart one, from deputy chief Warren Riley," I told Brown. "He says, 'One guy saw six bodies. Then another guy saw six bodies. And another guy saw the same six and all of a sudden, it becomes 18.'"

The broadcasters had a point about public officials fueling the rumor mill, a point we had made, but not dwelled on, in our original story. In the most extreme case, Nagin told Oprah Winfrey that people in the Dome had sunk to an "almost animalistic state" after "five days watching dead bodies, watching hooligans killing people, raping people."

Then–Police Chief Eddie Compass—pushed into retirement by Nagin immediately after our story broke—spoke of "babies" being raped.

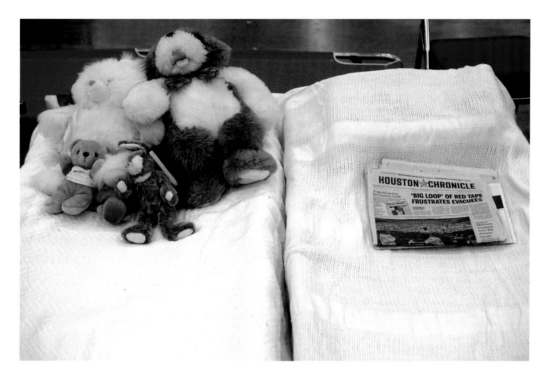

A copy of the local newspaper lies atop a cot being used by Hurricane Katrina evacuees living in the Astrodome in Houston on September 11, 2005. (© Ron Haviv/VII/ Corbis.)

Still, Brown got past the public-official bashing and grasped the point of our story that many others missed: It hadn't been an "investigation," as some termed it, but rather an explanatory piece. We never intended to write "gotcha" journalism or declare ourselves the holier-than-thou hometown paper, preaching to the rest of the media and the public officials we all quoted. We just wanted to get the story right, and explain, to the extent possible, how it came to be wrong. . . .

Pitfalls of the Twenty-Four-Hour News Cycle

Av Westin, a former vice president and executive producer for ABC News, says television reporters' and anchors' repeating of mythical violence, with sloppy attribution, marred otherwise remarkable journalism that aggressively reported the catastrophic damage of Katrina. He chalked it up to a lesson the television media should already have learned in the era of 24-hour news: Journalism requires thoughtful editing often absent in the competitive rush to air emotional breaking news.

> Journalism requires thoughtful editing often absent in the competitive rush to air emotional breaking news.

"When I was at ABC, nothing got on the air without having the piece read in to us," he says. "Now, they're on the air 24-7 and they have to fill airtime, and that leads frequently to the reporting of rumor and speculation.... Rather than saying, 'Let's wait five minutes,' they just go with it because it's in front of them. They keep learning that lesson and forgetting that lesson."

Then the mistakes feed off one another and multiply, Westin says. "There's something I call the 'out there syndrome'—it's okay for us to publish it because someone else already has, so it's 'out there,'" he says, rather than each media outlet confirming its own facts. "With 24-7 news, the deadline is always now, you go with whatever you've got, you stick it on the air."...

Correcting Misinformed News Coverage

As New Orleanians, playing a key role in correcting the international image of our own citizens gave us a deep satisfaction. Mostly poor, overwhelmingly African American, flood victims in the two shelters had been, in the most egregious cases, portrayed as beasts, raping and killing one another and even shooting at rescue workers trying to save them.

As journalists, reporting myths and later correcting them offers vital lessons on ramping up skepticism in initial reporting from chaotic environments—even if the sources are authoritative ones. We have three basic tools to use here, one during the reporting, the other during publishing, the third during any needed correction of initial reports.

The first is the persistent questioning of sources—about their sources: How do you know that? Did you see it? Who told you this? Are you 100 percent sure this happened? Who else can confirm it?

The second, wisely suggested in a column by former *Washington Post* Ombudsman Michael Getler, is careful and frequent qualification: "There is a journalistic device that is informative, accurate and protective, but that too often doesn't get used. It is a simple sentence that says: 'This account could not be independently verified.'"

The second time I wrote about the bodies in the freezer, as part of a narrative piece I penned for this magazine, I added just such a qualification (see "Apocalypse in New Orleans," October/November). At the time, a few days after I'd been to the Convention Center, I still had no higher-level confirmation of a body count—because no official count had been taken. So I added a sentence saying the presence and number of bodies at the center was "still unconfirmed amid a swirl of urban myths churned up by the storm."

The revision came as a result of a conversation with an editor in which I initially recommended cutting the mention of 40 bodies altogether unless I could confirm it independently before deadline. We compromised, adding the qualifier and strict attribution of the number to the guardsmen.

The third tool, which lately has been on display by many, though not all, media outlets, is an attitude that embraces the correcting of major news stories as news itself, not something to be buried in a corrections box.

"I think you treat it as a separate story, and it should have A1 prominence," says Hub Brown, an associate professor of broadcast journalism at the S.I. Newhouse School of Public Communications at Syracuse University. "Of course, print journalists are so much more meticulous at correcting their mistakes. . . . Why not have a segment in the newscast that says, 'We've reported this through the past day, and it turned out to be wrong'?"

That sort of record correction would be a lot less painful—indeed, not painful at all—if journalists' initial dispatches contained detailed attribution, especially for high-temperature reports out of disaster zones. With stories like Katrina, in which rock-solid information in many cases proved so elusive, that should extend even to the point of publishing exactly how official sources came to know the information in question. David Carr, a media columnist for the *New York Times*, was one of the first to question some of the early Katrina reporting in a September 19 column headlined: "More Horrible than Truth: News Reports."

> Stories that may have started with some basis in fact got exaggerated and distorted as they were passed orally.

While Carr, in his column and in an interview, asserted that the media should shoulder their share of the blame, he was stunned at the degree to which public officials solidified the myths. "In New Orleans, that's what set this apart" from other examples of misinformation reported by the media, he says. "I was actually prepared a week before and had a column set to go, but then I realized the top police official and the top elected official were confirming these rumors. So how could I go after reporters on the ground receiving confirmation that this happened?" . . .

While the media should learn lessons from Katrina, appropriate caution can't lead to paralysis. Backing off aggressive reporting of scenes where "official" information and sources, in some cases, literally don't exist isn't an option. The many early Katrina stories marred by exaggerations or errors still stand out as a point of pride for the media. The quick reaction to the storm by reporters put accounts—most of them true and confirmed—of dire suffering in the faces of the public and authorities, prompting them to take action that saved lives.

Race and Class Dynamics in Katrina Coverage

As the debate about misreported Katrina violence rolled though blogs and more mainstream outlets, a conventional wisdom emerged: White middle-class reporters only believed and reported atrocities because they were predisposed to accept the worst about poor, black flood victims.

The race and class dynamics here are far more complicated. Many of the worst stories were attributed to poor, black flood victims themselves, along with African American public officials.

Brown, the Syracuse professor and an African American who teaches about diversity in the media, says that's no surprise. Black people are sometimes unconsciously biased against black people, too. "The fact that racism exists in the country doesn't mean everybody of one race feels one way, and everybody of another race feels the other," he says. "Sometimes victims of racism believe the worst about themselves. That's part of what makes it so harmful."

[The] Poynter [Institute's Keith] Woods, an African American who has been writing and teaching about reporting on racial issues for years, doesn't buy the charge that the reports were driven largely by racial bias. It's not necessarily a gigantic leap in logic, he says, to believe that New Orleanians would murder one another in desperate times—they murder one another with regularity during normal times.

"I spent most of my life in the city of New Orleans, and when I left, it was the murder capital of the country," Woods says. "If you were to tell me a bunch of people murdered each other in the Dome and Convention Center, why wouldn't I believe it? . . . Race played a role, but it's an indecipherable role. It's useless trying to spend a lot of time trying to figure it out because you have to climb into the psyche of the people who were there."

You also have to deal in hypothetical comparisons. What would the media have reported if the Dome had been packed with white people?

The reality of being white in New Orleans and most of America, of course, substantially increases the likelihood of being middle class, and thus substantially decreases the likelihood of being anywhere near a shelter of any kind during a disaster of Katrina proportions.

I'll offer another hypothetical comparison that takes class out of the issue and leaves only race: If Katrina had hit a poor, white trailer-park town in, say, the Florida Panhandle, and white refugees and white public officials had offered the media tales of rape and murder, would any of us have doubted their "eyewitness" or "official" accounts?

There's no simple answer. White trailer-park towns don't typically include a Dome that might end up packed with about 30,000 people, with no power, no working toilets and scant medical care.

While the role of race can't be definitively measured, I have little doubt that, consciously or unconsciously, some white reporters and probably a smaller number of black ones found it more plausible that babies had been raped and children knifed in a black crowd than they would in a theoretical white one.

But I don't think race was the overriding factor.

I'm more inclined to go with an expanded version of Aaron Brown's gossip-line theory: that stories that may have started with some basis in fact got exaggerated and distorted as they were passed orally—often the only mode of communication—through extraordinarily frustrated and stressed multitudes of people, including refugees, cops, soldiers, public officials and, ultimately, the press.

The confusion was created by a titanic clash of communications systems. Stone-age storytelling got amplified by space-age technology. . . .

Journalists Kept Reporting

I can assure you that Mikel Brooks and his fellow guardsman sincerely believed what they told me. They talked to me out of disgust at the horrors, real and imagined. They did not "lie," which implies intent. They were consumed with a more important job at the time than nailing down every report they heard and believed: giving food and water to the living to keep them from joining the dead. It was my job to make sure what they said was true.

Ultimately, I followed up and did that job, as did many others. What Woods finds curious about the media-bashing on the Katrina story is that critics don't credit the media for doing the research to prove their early reports wrong.

"Don't forget, the journalists kept reporting—the reason you know that things were reported badly is because the journalists told you."

Media Coverage of Hurricane Katrina Was Too Focused on New Orleans

Daniel Rothschild

In the following viewpoint, a public policy expert contends that the media missed the full story in the wake of Hurricane Katrina. The disaster zone after the storm covered 90,000 square miles, the author asserts, and New Orleans encompasses 350 square miles of that area. Yet, he maintains, New Orleans received the majority of the news coverage. Instead of reporting on the Gulf Coast as a whole, the author says, the media chose to focus on New Orleans because it was easier to report. While there has been debate about inaccurate reporting in New Orleans, he says, areas outside of the city were left out of the coverage altogether. Daniel Rothschild is senior vice president and chief operating officer of the Mercatus Center at George Mason

University. From 2005 to 2009, he helped lead the center's Gulf
Coast Recovery Project.

Rather than deal with the nuances affecting communities in Louisiana, Mississippi, and Alabama,
the media like to cover New Orleans as if it is
synonymous with the entire area affected by Hurricane
Katrina. This is similar to the way the media often treats
"Africa" as if it were one extremely large, monolithic
country.

Many well-researched stories by dedicated reporters have come out of New Orleans in the past two years.
But what's largely missing is any coverage of the Louisi-
anan parishes near New Orleans, or of the many coun-
ties in Mississippi also hit by Katrina. In the aftermath
of Katrina, the Red Cross provided assistance to some
4 million people, although only 450,000 people lived in
New Orleans. President [George W.]
Bush's disaster declaration covered
90,000 square miles. New Orleans
encompasses only 350 square miles,
almost half of it water. Many parts of
New Orleans did not flood, but over
99 percent of buildings in neighboring St. Bernard Parish did.

> Reporters disproportionately focus on New Orleans because it's . . . both a simpler and more complex story than other areas damaged by Katrina.

New Orleans as the Most Interesting Story

Why, then, does New Orleans receive the majority of the
media coverage? Reporters disproportionately focus on
New Orleans because it's more interesting, it fits more
preconceived narratives, and it is, paradoxically, both a
simpler and more complex story than other areas damaged by Katrina.

The complexity stems from the diversity of experiences across New Orleans' neighborhoods and

communities. No single factor—be it financial resources, political power, geography, or demography—portends an area's post-Katrina experience. The wealthy Lakeview area, for example, took over a year to show any progress, while working-class Broadmoor began rebuilding within weeks. The previously apolitical, keep-to-themselves Vietnamese-American community in New Orleans East began rebuilding homes and packing their church for Mass before Entergy, the local power monopoly, would even turn their electricity back on. This complexity creates human interest stories, which reporters package into pre-imagined narratives of race, class, and power, even if the anecdotes don't fit what's actually happening.

But the New Orleans story is also simple, because it can be told through the lens of the same superficial, Disneyfied version of New Orleans that informed most Americans' conceptions of the city before Katrina. Few visitors to New Orleans ventured outside of the French Quarter, Business District, and Garden District. However, New Orleans as understood by the majority of its residents is more complex than an hour-long tour or weekend bender lets on. Since Katrina, reporters focus on telling stories through the tourism-and-jazz lens, despite the fact that before Katrina, shipping and related industries represented more income and more jobs than tourism. But the familiar stereotypes make for easy reporting.

> People in Mississippi and Louisiana locales outside New Orleans get almost no coverage at all.

New Orleans Was Not the Only Affected Area

New Orleans is still struggling, but it is not alone. For all the frustration people in New Orleans feel about warped or clichéd coverage, people in Mississippi and Louisiana locales outside New Orleans get almost no coverage at all. Across the Pearl River, Louisianans feel that Mississippians are getting more than their share of federal money. Key to making sense of this is understanding that Louisiana and Mississippi experienced very different storms.

Mississippi suffered hurricane damage. In many areas, Katrina's storm surge penetrated a mile inland, to the raised CSX railroad tracks, which act as a levee and broke much of the surge's power, and washed away virtually everything in its path. Further inland, homes and businesses were flooded and damaged by 140-mph winds. The destruction was significant—but St. Bernard Parish and the New Orleans' Lower Ninth Ward suffered more.

Orleans and St. Bernard Parishes in Louisiana were, by contrast, not victims of a traditional hurricane, but of poor government and central planning, which allowed massive but preventable flooding. In these areas, levees,

Extensive damage caused by Hurricane Katrina can be seen in Gulfport, Mississippi, on August 29, 2005. Some areas of the Gulf Coast that were devastated by the hurricane did not receive as much attention as New Orleans. (© Oscar Sosa/Bloomberg via Getty Images.)

floodwalls, and engineering projects designed to keep flooding out failed, and instead kept water in. For periods ranging from days to weeks, entire neighborhoods sat underwater, while antiquated city pumps slowly inched down the flooding. Mississippi was hit by a moderately sized hurricane, while Louisiana suffered from a flood of biblical proportions.

This crucial distinction is often lost in media coverage. That's unfortunate, because understanding it is vital to understanding the subsequent recovery efforts. Reporters and pundits sometimes distinguish Louisiana and Mississippi by noting the marked difference in the two states' recovery periods. Frequently, Mississippi's lower taxes, less generous welfare programs, and Republican leadership get credit for making the state less dependent on Washington, and therefore better able to pull itself up by the straps of its collective hip-waders. Many Mississippians that I and my colleagues have interviewed or spoken with have bought into this story—"we" are not like "them."

> Katrina's impact wasn't uniform across the Gulf Coast.

Lack of Uniformity in the Recovery Efforts

Truth be told, neither state is an exemplar of self-sufficiency or probity. According to the Tax Foundation, in 2004 Louisiana got back $1.45, while Mississippi received $1.77, for every dollar sent to Washington. Researchers Russell Sobel and Peter Leeson point out that while Louisiana does bear the ignominy of the highest rate of public corruption in the country, Mississippi isn't far behind. In other words, while differences exist, neither Mississippi nor Louisiana are paragons of virtuous—or limited—government.

The speed and quality of the recovery effort along the Gulf Coast have depended upon a number of factors: the type and amount of damage from the storm, insurance coverage on affected homes and businesses, whether governments made credible commitments about infrastructure and the "rules of the game" for rebuilding, and the inherent resilience of the communities affected. Indeed, community resilience is perhaps the most critical factor in recovery, and one that researchers are just beginning to understand.

The most effective solutions to rebuilding are actually coming from people, not governments. So it's not really prudent to discuss recovery in conventional, red-blue political geography. While governance is important, it hasn't been the sole or even primary determinant of the recovery process. What's happened since Katrina is far too complex for neatly-packaged conclusions about party or ideological supremacy, or to draw broad inferences about the nature of people in Mississippi, New Orleans, or those Louisianans outside of New Orleans.

Scholars will undoubtedly debate the legacy of Katrina for decades, and we will hopefully learn a great deal about the role that politics and public policy played in the recovery process. But even today, two things are evident: Political geography is not the silver bullet for explaining the response to disasters, and Katrina's impact wasn't uniform across the Gulf Coast.

Structural Racism Hindered the Response to Hurricane Katrina

Kristin E. Henkel, John F. Dovidio, and Samuel L. Gaertner

In the following viewpoint, researchers examine the role of racism in the aftermath of Hurricane Katrina. Some have argued that the ineffectual hurricane response was due to overt racism on behalf of government officials; however, the authors maintain this assertion oversimplifies the situation. They find that many of the tragic consequences that impacted black residents in New Orleans were the result of historical factors and institutional discrimination. At the time this viewpoint was written, Kristin E. Henkel was a PhD candidate in social psychology at the University of Connecticut; John F. Dovidio was a professor of psychology at the University of Connecticut; and Samuel L. Gaertner was a professor of psychology at the University of Delaware.

SOURCE. Kristin E. Henkel, John F. Dovidio, and Samuel L. Gaertner, "Institutional Discrimination, Individual Racism, and Hurricane Katrina," *Analyses of Social Issues and Public Policy*, vol. 6, no. 1, 2006, pp. 100, 105–108. Reproduced with permission of Blackwell Publishing in the format Republish in a book via Copyright Clearance Center. All rights reserved.

In the aftermath of Hurricane Katrina, which devastated New Orleans and had particular impact on its Black community in August of 2005, accusations pertaining to the lack of preparation for the storm and for the plight of its victims were heatedly exchanged. Racism was one focus of the debate. On one side, it was asserted that the inadequate response to the storm and the flooding was due to obvious racism. This sentiment is evident in a statement by Kanye West, a prominent rap artist, who said, "[President] George Bush doesn't care about Black people." In response and in contrast, others such as Secretary of State Condoleezza Rice adamantly denied that race had anything to do with Hurricane Katrina or the government's response to it. She claimed that "nobody, especially the President, would have left people unattended on the basis of race."

From a social psychological perspective, both sides appeared to oversimplify the situation, and polemics obscured the potential roles of historical factors, institutional discrimination, and contemporary subtle forms of individual racism, all of which likely played parts in the impact of Hurricane Katrina and the government's response to it. This [viewpoint] examines some events and decisions related to Hurricane Katrina, and explores how historical and contemporary orientations toward Blacks in the United States likely shaped responses in a way that produced particularly tragic consequences for Black residents of New Orleans without overt antipathy or intention of decision makers. We emphasize the importance of how the past shapes contemporary race relations. In the next section, we provide a brief overview of the forces that contribute to racism in the United States. We then apply these psychological insights into the dynamics of racism to understand the events and decisions that produced uniquely devastating outcomes for Blacks in New Orleans. We conclude by exploring the implications of this analysis for specific interventions in New Orleans and for policy more generally.

It is impossible to know whether the processes we propose were operating among the protagonists; we can only point out that the immenseness of the devastation created tremendous confusion and communication problems and, further, show that these are precisely the conditions most conducive to the activation of these processes. We have prepared this [viewpoint] in the interests of helping people sort through the different perspectives on these tragic events and to sensitize policy makers, officials, and future rescuers to how racial factors can play a role during such catastrophes. . . .

What happened during and after Hurricane Katrina was determined not only by the present circumstances on the Gulf Coast but also by a history of discriminatory policies and practices, particularly in the New Orleans area, that created socioeconomic and consequent housing disparities along racial lines. In addition, although the actions of decision makers during Hurricane Katrina and its aftermath may have appeared "colorblind," without particular sensitivity to the unique vulnerabilities of the Black population these actions were subtly biased and produced racially disparate consequences. Also, historical discrimination and contemporary institutional racism eroded the trust of Blacks in New Orleans for the government, which adversely influenced the effectiveness of interventions in the aftermath of Hurricane Katrina. In this section we therefore examine the influences of (a) historical discrimination and contemporary institutional racism, (b) subtle bias at the individual level, and (c) interracial distrust.

> "What happened during and after Hurricane Katrina was determined . . . also by a history of discriminatory policies."

Historical Discrimination, Contemporary Institutional Racism, and Hurricane Katrina

The impact by Hurricane Katrina was catastrophic by all measures. Besides billions of dollars of damage and a premier city in the United States left largely in ruins, between 1,100 and 1,700 people died and thousands more are still unaccounted for. In addition, Hurricane Katrina was particularly devastating for Blacks. The flooding caused by the hurricane was particularly damaging to Black neighborhoods, communities that were relatively uninsured against floods. Thus, many of the Blacks in New Orleans who survived but were displaced by Hurricane Katrina will not be able to afford to return to the city and to the areas where they once lived.

To understand what happened during Katrina and why it had such a disproportionate negative impact on Blacks, it is important to appreciate the local and national historical context that surrounded the disaster. One of the most significant legacies of slavery and historical discrimination in the United States is the pervasive racial disparity in wealth. The median family income for Whites in 1994 was $33,600 but was only $20,508 for Blacks. Blacks' incomes were only 62% of Whites' incomes. Moreover, when net worth is considered, weighing family financial assets and debts, the gap is even greater. In 1994, the median net worth for Whites was $52,944 as compared to $6,723 for Blacks. That is, Blacks' net worth was only 12% of Whites' net worth.

> "Fewer available resources meant that it may not have been as easy for Blacks, who were less likely to own cars, to leave the city."

Contemporary biases further contribute to racial disparities in income. Minority groups have disproportionate difficulty finding jobs as compared to majority groups: based on job audits across several countries, minority-

Various Minorities Suffered Greatly Because of Hurricane Katrina

One of the untold stories of Katrina is how the hurricane impacted racial and ethnic minorities other than blacks. For instance, nearly 40,000 Mexican citizens who lived (mostly in trailers) and worked in New Orleans were displaced. Altogether, nearly 145,000 Mexicans in the entire Gulf Coast region were scattered by Katrina. Latinos make up 3 percent of Louisiana's population, 124,222 people of the state's 4,515,770 residents. Many Latinos who live in the South are foreign born and are undocumented laborers on farms or in hotels, restaurants, and other service industry jobs.

The fear that government officials and police would target undocumented immigrants discouraged many Latinos from seeking hurricane relief. . . . Thousands of Native Americans on the Gulf Coast were hard hit by the storm as well. According to the National Congress of American Indians (NCAI), several Native American tribes were in harm's way across the damaged region. . . . For one tribe near Chalmette, Louisiana, the local high school served as a tribal morgue, holding the bodies of Native American workers, including shrimpers and other fishermen, who were drowned in the flooding near New Orleans. The Mississippi Band of Choctaw Indians experienced power outages on their

group members have a 23.7 percent chance of being discriminated against when applying for any given job. Even when Blacks find jobs, they are overrepresented in jobs with poor working conditions, such as shift work, long hours, repetitive tasks, physical dangers, and accident rates. They also have disproportionately low mobility out of such low-end jobs. Institutional discrimination in the labor market only serves to increase discrepancies between minority group and majority group members. Discrepancies in the labor market lead to a disproportionate number of Blacks in positions of lower socioeconomic status.

Race and racial disparities are particularly relevant for understanding the impact of Hurricane Katrina in reservation and sought shelter at tribal hotels. The NCAI partnered with the National Indian Gaming Association (NIGA) to raise relief funds for Native Americans in the Gulf States.

There were also nearly 50,000 Vietnamese fishermen who labored on the Louisiana coast—while others worked in the service and manufacturing industries—along with a large contingent of Filipino American shrimpers, part of the oldest Filipino community in North America. A community of Vietnamese shrimpers also lived and worked near Mississippi; many of them were displaced, while others died in the horrible pounding of Katrina. There were nearly 30,000 Vietnamese evacuees dispersed to Houston, although many of them were denied entry into the Astrodome, finding shelter instead at Houston's Hong Kong City Mall.

The oversight of Latino, Native American, and Vietnamese and Filipino suffering in the catastrophe not only reinforces for the latter three groups their relative invisibility in American culture, and for Latinos their relative marginalization in the region. It shows as well that our analysis of minorities must constantly be revised to accommodate a broader view of how race and ethnicity function in the culture.

SOURCE. *Michael Eric Dyson,* Come Hell or High Water: Hurricane Katrina and the Color of Disaster. *New York: Perseus, 2006.*

New Orleans. For example, in the context of Hurricane Katrina, fewer available resources meant that it may not have been as easy for Blacks, who were less likely to own cars, to leave the city. In addition, socioeconomic differences influenced the vulnerability of Blacks, relative to Whites, to the devastating consequences of Hurricane Katrina. Approximately one-third of the population in the New Orleans metropolitan area is Black, ranking it 11th in terms of percentage of Black population among over 300 major metropolitan areas in the United States. The largest proportion of Blacks is concentrated within the city limits, representing 68% of the population, many of whom lived in the most low-lying areas—those most vulnerable to Hurricane Katrina. In addition, New Orleans historically has been one of the cities with the largest racial disparities in income and wealth. It showed the fourth largest increase in racial disparity in income in recent years. The poverty rate in New Orleans has been almost twice the national rate, and a third of Blacks and half of the Black children in the city live below the poverty level. This racial gap in income and wealth contributed significantly to the particular vulnerability of Blacks in New Orleans to Hurricane Katrina.

One consequence of racial disparities in wealth and income, which is exacerbated by contemporary housing discrimination, is the residential segregation of Blacks. In general, more affluent residential areas in the United States are predominantly, if not virtually exclusively, White. Thus, access to housing in these areas requires either pre-existing wealth or access to substantial housing loans. As we noted earlier, the racial gap in wealth is even greater than the sizable income disparity. Moreover, in part due to their lower wealth and available assets, Blacks have more difficulty obtaining housing loans than do Whites. In 2001, 36% of Black applicants, compared to 16% of White applicants, were denied conventional home mortgage loans. However, even when controlling for financial status, Blacks are denied home loans at rates much greater than Whites. Among applicants who had incomes less than 50% of the income for the local area, Blacks were denied loans 42.7% of the time, whereas Whites were denied 29.6% of the time. Among the applicants who made more than 120% of the median income, Blacks were denied 19.6% of the time, whereas Whites were denied only 6.8% of the time.

Institutional policies, past and present, have further contributed to residential segregation of Blacks and Whites. According to [lawyer Marc] Seitles, federal and state governments have had large roles in creating and maintaining residential racial segregation. For example, the Federal Housing Administration (FHA) employed practices that disadvantaged Blacks since it began in 1937. It used a practice called "redlining" to determine risks associated with loans made to borrowers in specific neighborhoods. "Red-lining" involved rating neighborhoods such that the neighborhoods in the top two categories were White, stable, and in demand. The "high risk" categories involved Blacks. The third category was made up of working class neighborhoods near Black residences, and the fourth category was Black neighborhoods. As a result of this policy, most mortgages and home loans went to middle class White families, promoting the racial segregation of neighborhoods, particularly in urban areas. Further, the federal government used interstate highway and urban renewal programs to increase segregation.

> In New Orleans poor Black neighborhoods were on lower, undesirable, cheaper land that was particularly vulnerable to flooding.

In addition to institutional discrimination rooted in historical practices, contemporary biases conspire to contribute further to residential segregation. [Sociology professors Mary J. Fischer and Douglas S. Massey] found that callers identifiable as Black were systematically discriminated against relative to those identifiable as White in housing inquiries, controlling for the socioeconomic status of the caller. The primary exception to this effect was for Black neighborhoods. Blacks were more likely than Whites to gain access to areas that already had high concentrations of Blacks. Thus, institutional discrimination, along with individual discrimination, tends to deny Blacks access to the more affluent neighborhoods, which are much more readily available to Whites. Due to past and present institutional discrimination in housing and mortgage processes, neighborhoods are segregated and mortgages go to largely White neighborhoods, which only perpetuates the problem.

The history of racial disparities in income and wealth and the influence of institutional discrimination have had a significant influence on housing patterns in New Orleans. New Orleans currently ranks 29th out of 318 metropolitan areas examined in terms of the extent of neighborhood racial segregation, and the highest concentrations of Blacks have been in poorer areas. In addition, as [former first lady] Laura Bush observed, in New Orleans poor Black neighborhoods were on lower, undesirable, cheaper land that was particularly vulnerable to flooding. As a function of where they lived, when Hurricane Katrina hit, many Black people in New Orleans were already in a position to be disproportionately affected by the disaster. For example, HUD-funded [US Department of Housing and Urban Development] public housing units above Feret Street West, which were occupied largely by Blacks, and New Orleans East were also on lower ground more vulnerable to flooding than higher, more desirable neighborhoods. Even areas that Blacks considered attractive locations within the city, such as New Orleans East and the Lower Ninth Ward, were at environmental risk. New Orleans East is home to middle income Blacks who left the urban center of New Orleans in the 1960s and 1970s to build affordable homes in this area. The homes were affordable because they were built on slabs and were located 2.5 to 4.0 feet below sea level. The Lower Ninth Ward is a neighborhood of primarily modest houses, often the location of choice of musicians and multi-generational Black families of the metropolitan area. It is situated in close proximity to an industrial canal, which posed particular health risks during the flood. This neighborhood was devastated by Hurricanes Betsy [1965] and Rita [September 2005], as well as by Hurricane Katrina.

In summary, the result of the institutional discrimination in New Orleans as outlined here is multifaceted. Because of discriminatory housing and mortgage policies and practices, Blacks tended to live in more environmentally vulnerable areas of the city. The discrepancies in socioeconomic status were exacerbated by discrimination in the labor market, which on the whole prevented Blacks from gaining jobs, specifically ones of higher status, and prevented acquisition of material resources, such as personal cars, that would have enabled them to evacuate New Orleans for safer areas as Hurricane Katrina approached. When evacuation orders were announced, a disproportionate number of Blacks in the areas most at-risk lacked the resources to leave the city. "Many of them were people without automobiles," explained Marc Morial, former mayor of New Orleans and now the president and chief executive officer of the National Urban League. They were "people who couldn't afford a hotel room, who may have had no choice but to remain. And that means that the people who remain in New Orleans are disproportionately poor people, disproportionately African-American." Past and recent institutional discrimination on the basis of race thus contributed to the particular vulnerability of the Black population of New Orleans to a disaster like Hurricane Katrina.

Kindness Trumped Chaos After Hurricane Katrina

Rebecca Solnit

The author of the following viewpoint examines the positive outcomes of Hurricane Katrina. Although the storm had tragic consequences, a surge of empathy arose as well, she writes, noting that the disaster brought a swell of volunteers and activists who helped rebuild the area. The survivors of the storm found a solidarity through the crisis, the author says, which fostered a sense of empowerment and resilience. Rebecca Solnit is a writer, historian, and activist. She is the author of numerous books, including *A Paradise Built in Hell: The Extraordinary Communities That Arise in Disaster* and *Hope in the Dark*.

T he taxi driver called me "girlfriend" and "sweetheart" with the familiar sweetness of New Orleanians, so I figured I could ask a few personal questions. He was from the Lower Ninth Ward, one of the neighborhoods inundated by Katrina—a mostly poor, mostly black edge of the city isolated and imperiled by two manmade canals—and it had taken him three and a half years to return to New Orleans. He still wasn't in his neighborhood, but he was back in the city, and his family was back, and they were determined to come back all the way.

What happened in the aftermath of Hurricane Katrina is more remarkable than almost anyone has told. More than a million volunteers came to New Orleans to gut houses, rebuild, and stand in solidarity with the people who endured not just a hurricane but a deluge of [President George W.] Bush Administration incompetence and institutionalized racism at all levels of government, which temporarily turned the drowned city into a prison. Supplies were not allowed in by a panicky government; people were not allowed out, and a wholly unnatural crisis ensued.

> " I have again and again met passionate young activists who intended to come for a week or a month and never left. "

Hurricane Katrina Led to a Wave of Solidarity

Even so, an astounding wave of solidarity and empathy arose. At Hurricanehousing.org more than 200,000 people volunteered to shelter evacuees, often in their own homes. And then there were those legions of volunteers, many of them white, working in a city that had been two-thirds black. . . . I have again and again met passionate young activists who intended to come for a week or a month and never left. In the Lower Ninth, my taxi driver's neighborhood, things looked better than even six months before. [Actor] Brad Pitt's Make It Right Foundation now has dozens of solar-powered homes, built on stilts for the next inundation, scattered across the lowlands of the neighborhood. New businesses have opened on St. Claude Avenue, the main thoroughfare, and children play in the once-abandoned streets.

It's hard to say that there is a recipe for solidarity across race and class lines. During crises, the official reaction from government and media is often widespread fear—based on a belief that in the absence of institutional authority people revert to Hobbesian[1] selfishness and violence, or just feckless conduct. Scholars Lee Clarke and Karon Chess call this fear of the public, particularly the poor and nonwhite public, "elite panic." Because these "elites" shape reaction as well as opinion, their beliefs can be deadly.

> What gets called recovery can constitute the counter-revolution—the taking back of power.

But the truth is that most people are altruistic, resourceful, and constructive during crisis. A disaster is actually threatening to elites, not because the response is selfish but because it often unfolds like a revolution, in which the status quo has evaporated.

Disasters Evaporate the Status Quo

Civil society improvises its own systems of survival —community kitchens, clinics, neighborhood councils, and networks of volunteers and survivors—often decentralized and deeply empowering for the individuals involved. What gets called recovery can constitute the counter-revolution—the taking back of power.

Perhaps the biggest question for a disaster like Katrina is to what extent this transformed sense of self and society lasts and matters: Can it be a foundation for a stronger civil society, more solidarity, and grassroots power? It has been so in many ways in New Orleans, with groups like the Common Ground Clinic—a free health clinic that was started days after the hurricane and is still going strong five years later.

One important tool for future disasters, and social change in the absence of disaster, is simply knowledge of what really happened: how many people in the hours, days, weeks and months after Katrina behaved with courage, love, and creativity, and how much they constituted the majority response. Such human capacities can be an extraordinary resource not just in crisis but in realizing our dearest hopes for a stronger society and more meaningful lives.

What gets called recovery can constitute the counterrevolution—the taking back of power.

Katrina is hardly a happy story. More than 1,600 people died. The racism on the part of the media, the authorities ready to believe any rumor, and the vigilantes who took it upon themselves to regard any black man as a looter and to administer the death penalty for these imagined minor property crimes were a reminder of how ugly this country can be and how much remains to be done. The city used the disaster as an excuse to shut down most of the public housing even though much of it was undamaged and intact housing was desperately needed.

Poverty continues, and so does racism; the South did not stop being the South or America America. And the BP [oil] spill menaces the region in a way that is even more ominous than Katrina. The hurricane was after all a kind of event that has come ashore for tens of thousands of years, and when it was over people could rebuild. What can be done to ameliorate the spill is still a mystery, and the coastal edge of Louisiana, with its diverse fishing and foraging cultures and its abundance of wildlife, is poisoned.

New Orleans Will Never Be the Same

New Orleans will never be quite the city it was. People there lost what many of us have not had for generations: deep roots in place, a strong sense of culture, and an intricate web of social ties to family and community, whether it's a church, Mardi Gras krewe, musical group, black social aid and pleasure club, or neighborhood group. Much was reclaimed; many returned, but some did not or cannot.

The taxi driver took us to the New Orleans Convention Center, where so many people, mostly African American, had been stranded in the days after Hurricane Katrina. But that day in July [2010], it was hosting the Essence Festival, a black music festival at which tens of thousands of people in summer splendor circulated. Among the mix of booths were several from organizations founded during the weeks and months after the storm but still going strong.

Traveling through a vibrant New Orleans not quite five years [2010] after the city was pronounced dead means understanding what dedication, will, solidarity, and love can achieve. This year of disasters—the earthquakes in Haiti and Chile, the volcano in Iceland, the spill in the Gulf, the floods and heat waves and droughts and rising waters—remind all of us that we are entering an era where disaster will be common and intense. Survival will be grounded in understanding our own capacity for power and resilience, creativity, and solidarity.

Note

1. A theory by philosopher Thomas Hobbes that self-preservation is a natural instinct that can lead people and nations to attack others out of fear.

Uneven Katrina Recovery Efforts Often Offered the Most Help to the Most Affluent

Michael A. Fletcher

In the following viewpoint, a journalist examines recovery efforts in the Gulf Coast five years after Hurricane Katrina. The state governments in Louisiana and Mississippi have structured recovery programs in ways that help the most affluent residents, he says. The author finds that the recovery is uneven, and those who were well off before the storm have fared better than those who were struggling prior to the hurricane. Years later, he writes, the lives of many New Orleans residents are still disrupted by the storm. Michael A. Fletcher is a national economics correspondent for the *Washington Post* and coauthor of *Supreme Discomfort: The Divided Soul of Clarence Thomas*.

The massive government effort to repair the damage from Hurricane Katrina is fostering a stark divide as the state governments in Louisiana and Mississippi structured the rebuilding programs in ways that often offered the most help to the most affluent residents.

The result, advocates say, has been an uneven recovery, with whites and middle-class people more likely than blacks and low-income people to have rebuilt their lives in the five years since the horrific storm.

> There is a sharp disparity in how residents view the pace of recovery.

"The recovery is really the tale of two recoveries," said James Perry, executive director of the Greater New Orleans Fair Housing Action Center. "For people who were well off before the storm, they are more likely to be back in their homes, back in their jobs and to have access to good health care. For those who were poor or struggling to get by before the storm, the opposite is true."

Louisiana's program to distribute grants to property owners whose homes were damaged or destroyed by Katrina was found by a federal judge this month [August 2010] to discriminate against black homeowners.

Disparities in the Pace of Recovery

Meanwhile, in Mississippi, state officials refused to offer rebuilding grants to property owners who suffered wind damage, explaining that the property owners should have carried private insurance. That rule hit low-income and black homeowners particularly hard, advocates say, because many of them were uninsured, often because they owned property that was passed down through the generations.

The $143 billion federally funded reconstruction effort, one of the largest such projects in the country's history, fortified vulnerable levees, rebuilt hundreds of public buildings, reconstructed miles of roads and bridges, and provided tens of thousands of residents with money to help piece together their shattered lives.

WHO RETURNED HOME AFTER KATRINA?

Percentage of evacuees who had returned to their pre-Katrina residence by October 2006.

Characteristic	Percent Who Returned to Residence	Percent Who Did Not Return to Residence
Race/ethnicity		
White	73.2%	26.8%
Black	48.5%	51.5%
Asian	80.7%	19.3%
Hispanic	57.1%	42.9%
Other race	42.9%	57.1%
Educational attainment		
Less than high school	59.3%	40.7%
High school	72.5%	27.5%
Some college	64.9%	35.1%
College	70.3%	29.7%

Taken from: Jeffrey A. Groen and Anne E. Polivka, "Hurricane Katrina Evacuees: Who They Are, Where They Are, and How They Are Faring," *Monthly Labor Review*, March 2008. www.bls.gov/opub/mlr/2008/03/art3full.pdf.

But there is a sharp disparity in how residents view the pace of recovery. A recent poll [August 13, 2010] by the Kaiser Family Foundation found that while seven in 10 New Orleans residents say the rebuilding process is "going in the right direction," a third say their lives are still disrupted by the storm.

African Americans are more than twice as likely as whites to say they have not yet recovered after Katrina, the survey found. And blacks in the city are 2½ times as likely to be low-income than whites.

"I just knew we had a rotten deal," said Edward Randolph, a disabled Vietnam veteran who with his wife, Angela, has been struggling to rebuild their duplex in New Orleans East. "We know we have a lot to do, but we just do not have the money to do it."

The storm propelled them on a years-long odyssey through Port Arthur, Tex., Houston and Arkansas. They did not return to their still-damaged home until 2008.

> Many of the most obvious scars from the catastrophe are healing.

The federally funded rebuilding program established by Louisiana officials—called Road Home—offered homeowners grants of up to $150,000. But homeowners could not collect more than the pre-storm value of their homes, regardless of the cost of repairs.

The Randolph home was valued at just $135,000, although repair costs were estimated by the state to be $308,000. The Randolphs were awarded a grant of $16,649, to supplement just over $100,000 they received in insurance payments.

This month, a federal judge ruled that the program's formula for calculating grants discriminates against black homeowners, who tend to live in neighborhoods with lower home values.

"We obviously disagree with the judge's action, which has stopped us from paying out some grants, and already have appealed it," said Christina Stephens, a spokes-woman for the Road Home program. "I think it is worth noting that the state did not create this program in a vacuum—the federal government signed off on the design of the program and any major changes we made along the way."

She added that the state has modified the program to pay out an additional $2 billion to more than 45,000 low-income homeowners. Overall, Road Home paid $8.6 billion to more than 127,000 homeowners.

Awaiting a Presidential Visit

Many of these simmering issues will not be visible when President [Barack] Obama arrives here Sunday [August 29, 2010] to mark the fifth anniversary of the storm that killed more than 1,800, uprooted more than 1 million Gulf Coast residents, and left 80 percent of this city submerged.

The visit is expected to underscore the president's support for a region still reeling not just from Katrina but from the largest oil spill in the nation's history, which is threatening the region's immediate economic future. A regional group of business and political leaders formed a coalition this week aimed at holding Obama to his promise to restore the Gulf Coast.

Obama's visit will also underscore the strides made since the breached floodwalls and overtopped levees left people here camping on highway overpasses, cowering in attics and retreating to the squalor of the Superdome and the Convention Center to escape the deadly waters.

The surreal landscape of grounded boats, washed-up appliances and mud-choked streets is long gone, and many of the most obvious scars from the catastrophe are healing. The Army Corps of Engineers has rebuilt 220 miles of levees and floodwalls.

The school system, widely viewed as one of the nation's worst before the storm, has been reborn with many charter schools. Though activists have filed a lawsuit alleging that special-needs students are being underserved by the new education structure, 59 percent of city students are in schools that meet state academic standards—more than double the number who attended such schools before Katrina.

The storm ravaged the city's hospital system, leaving many residents in the largely black eastern part of the city a long ambulance ride from emergency health care. At the same time, more than 90 neighborhood health clinics opened and are showing promise at delivering preventive care and helping people manage chronic diseases such as diabetes and hypertension.

But there is concern that many of the health centers, funded with federal grant money that is winding down,

Modern houses built by actor Brad Pitt's Make It Right project sit near a new section of levee wall in the Lower Ninth Ward of New Orleans five years after Hurricane Katrina. (© Rod Lamkey Jr./AFP/Getty Images.)

are struggling to draw enough insured patients to become self-sufficient.

"Everyone now has to transition to a more sustainable model of health care," said Sarat Raman, associate medical director of Daughters of Charity Services of New Orleans, which operates three clinics that serve 15,000 patients in the area. "You have to have a balance of patients."

Along Mississippi's Gulf Coast, where the violent winds and an unprecedented storm surge overwhelmed homeowners, sheared off roofs and splintered houses, the scene has also improved.

The waterfront casinos that provide a large chunk of this state's revenue are humming. The vast majority of residents are back in their rebuilt homes, although thousands are still struggling to find affordable housing because their recovery checks did not cover the cost of the damage.

> [New Orleans'] population drop has been most severe in black neighborhoods, many of which absorbed Katrina's most brutal blows.

Gaps Remain in the Recovery Process

Despite the improvements, many gaps remain.

The New Orleans area has regained more than 90 percent of its pre-Katrina population, according to the Greater New Orleans Community Data Center.

But in the city itself, just 78 percent of the population has returned, and a growing share of the region's poor now reside in the suburbs. The city's population drop has been most severe in black neighborhoods, many of which absorbed Katrina's most brutal blows.

Despite well-publicized recovery efforts, including a plan led by actor Brad Pitt to build 150 solar-powered homes, just 24 percent of the Lower Ninth Ward's pre-storm population has returned. There, newly rebuilt homes stand next to vacant lots or crumbling houses. Entire blocks remain desolate five years after the storm.

In middle-class Pontchartrain Park, not far from historically black Dillard University, just 55 percent of households have rebuilt, according to the data center.

Beyond the problems with Road Home, New Orleans has experienced a dramatic spike in rental costs since the storm.

"Many low-cost apartments are gone with the wind and the water," said Laura Tuggle, the outgoing managing attorney of Southeast Louisiana Legal Services. "Now, we're left with New York rents on New Orleans wages."

In Mississippi, where Katrina severely damaged more than 101,000 housing units, many residents face what advocates call a similar inequity. Praised in the aftermath of Katrina for his can-do attitude, Gov. Haley Barbour (R) received a series of waivers from the [President George W.] Bush administration that largely freed Mississippi from the requirement to spend at least half of his state's $5.5 billion in federal block grant money on low- and moderate-income residents.

> The more than $3 billion distributed by the state's housing recovery program went disproportionately to more-affluent residents.

Barbour successfully argued that the waivers were necessary to give the state flexibility to deal effectively with the widespread devastation.

That allowed the state to divert close to $1 billion to help devastated utilities rebuild, to subsidize residents' insurance premiums and to help fund the port and other economic development projects. Meanwhile, advocates say that more than 5,000 low-income Mississippi families have yet to settle in permanent housing since the storm.

State officials say they are expanding the number of public housing units beyond pre-Katrina levels and establishing programs to encourage development of affordable rental housing.

Still, advocates say the more than $3 billion distributed by the state's housing recovery program went disproportionately to more-affluent residents. The plan paid up to $150,000 to homeowners whose properties were damaged by the unprecedented storm surge spawned by Katrina, but nothing to those whose homes suffered wind damage.

A Funding Formula Discriminates Against Certain Homeowners

To be eligible for the initial grants, families had to have homeowners insurance, although the state later devised a program that paid grants of up to $100,000 to low-income, uninsured homeowners whose properties were damaged by the storm surge.

The rationale, state officials said, was that responsible homeowners had no way to know that they should have flood insurance in areas that federal experts deemed to be outside the flood plain.

"The storm surge was the priority," said Lee Youngblood, communications director of the Mississippi Development Authority. "Mississippi had no intention of compensating people who chose, for whatever reason, not to have wind insurance."

That formula struck some advocates as discriminatory. "The criteria discriminated against black storm victims, who more likely than not were renters, or, if homeowners, more likely than not lacked insurance," said Reilly Morse, co-director of housing policy for the Mississippi Center for Justice.

The state's formula had the effect of freezing out people whose homes were destroyed by the wind, which along much of the Mississippi coast meant black residents who often lived in paid-off homes that had been handed down through the generations. The expensive waterfront property was mostly owned by whites, while inland property, which suffered more wind damage, was owned largely by blacks.

In Gulfport [Mississippi], a railroad embankment that has long served as an informal racial demarcation line became a levee when Katrina hit.

As the surging waters crashed through their patio door and rose five feet in their home, a white couple, Ernest and Doreen Chamberlain, gathered their family and sought refuge on the black side of the tracks.

Coming upon an old, wood-frame house he thought was abandoned, Ernest Chamberlain began trying to break the door down, only to be surprised when it was opened by Irene Walker, an elderly black woman.

"She was like, 'Mister, what are you doing?'" he recalled. "Then she invited us in."

That's where the Chamberlains rode out the storm, even as raw sewage backed up into the Walker home.

Five years later, the Chamberlains are back in their sunny home. Although they had to fight with insurers and contractors, they secured a $150,000 grant from the state to help repair the flood damage, which totaled nearly $200,000.

Meanwhile, the Walker home sits abandoned. A church group installed a new roof, but the interior remains untouched. The 82-year-old Walker, meanwhile, is living with family members a few miles away.

"She hasn't gotten any help from the government for the house," said Occelletta Norwood, Walker's niece. "She got a little money from FEMA [Federal Emergency Management Agency] at the start, but that was it."

The Rebuilt New Orleans Levee System Is Inadequate

Bob Marshall

In the following viewpoint, a journalist reports on the rebuilt levee system in New Orleans. Almost a decade after the storm, the author writes, the US Army Corps of Engineers has finalized a $14.5 billion storm protection system for New Orleans. While the new system is superior to the one previously in place, some engineers and storm experts question whether it is an effective source of protection for the city. Critics of the new levee system argue that it should have been built to a higher standard in preparation for more severe storms in the future. Bob Marshall is a Pulitzer Prize–winning journalist who covers environmental issues for *The Lens* and has also worked as a reporter for the *Times-Picayune*.

As the U.S. Army Corps of Engineers puts the finishing touches on its new, $14.5 billion storm protection system for New Orleans, agency and local officials see the best protection the city has ever had.

But some engineers and storm experts familiar with the system's history see something else. Something less.

They see a system that after Hurricane Katrina was downgraded by Congress from one that had to be strong enough to repel the "most severe" storm to one that only had to qualify for flood insurance, a much lower standard.

> 'The corps has rebuilt a system to a lower standard of protection than its poorly built system that collapsed during Hurricane Katrina.'

"It's as if your poorly built, three-story house collapsed, so the contractor said, 'Ok, I'll replace it with a well-made, two-story house,'" said Mark Davis, director of the Tulane Institute on Water Resources Law & Policy.

"The corps has rebuilt a system to a lower standard of protection than its poorly built system that collapsed during Hurricane Katrina," Davis said.

Building to a Lower Standard

Is the storm protection system around New Orleans better than the old one? "Absolutely," Davis said. "Is it what we were supposed to have? No."

That shift has had two important effects, Davis and others say:

It lowered the design height of walls defending a city located on a sinking delta during an age of rising sea levels.

And it changed the purpose of the system from protecting lives to protecting property—a lesser challenge for designers.

"That's what Congress did" in directing the corps to build to a lesser standard, Davis said, "and that's not what the law says they must do. People should be asking the city, the state, and their representatives in Congress how this happened. Someone should be telling that story."

It's a story about an agency's reluctance to change course, a Congress on a budget-cutting mission and a city in a hurry to recover from disaster.

A History of the Levee System

It begins in 1965 when Congress, alarmed by the devastation Hurricane Betsy caused in and around New Orleans, passed a bill authorizing the Lake Pontchartrain and Vicinity Hurricane Protection Project—Public Law 89-298.

According to the law, the system was supposed to be strong enough to repel a storm consisting of "the most severe combination of meteorological conditions that are considered reasonably characteristic of the region."

That language comes from a government report that defined the Standard Project Hurricane, a model storm used by the Corps of Engineers to determine the height of the walls and levees around New Orleans.

The corps said such a storm would be so severe it was likely to occur only once every 200 years along the Louisiana coast.

The law was amended seven times from 1974 to 2000, but the standard of protection was never changed.

Forty years later, what the corps had built failed during Katrina, suffering about 50 breaches. Most were not the result of levees being overwhelmed by storm surge. More than 1,500 people were killed.

New Research, Same Tactics

Post-disaster investigations catalogued a long list of engineering mistakes and errors in judgment by the corps that contributed to the disaster.

> *Investigations catalogued a long list of engineering mistakes and errors in judgment by the corps that contributed to the disaster.*

One of the most troubling was the refusal by corps officials to upgrade their design as new information indicated that land was sinking faster and storms could be worse than originally predicted.

Even when new data increased the threat in the definition of the "most severe conditions," the corps claimed that the project could continue to use the standard set forth in 1965.

That happened at least twice.

In 1979 the National Weather Service alerted the corps to new research that showed the Standard Project Hurricane could be worse than previously expected.

The corps had originally described the model storm as a fast-moving Category 3 on the Saffir-Simpson scale. In 2006 Louisiana hurricane experts said the increases would make the Standard Project Hurricane at least a Category 4.

The corps never bumped up its specifications to account for the increased threat.

Indeed, an analysis conducted of project decisions by the Corps of Engineers in 2008 admits this was a grievous misstep, saying the decision meant the system no longer provided surge protection for the Standard Project Hurricane, a 200-year storm.

In 1985, the National Geodetic Survey told the corps that a new method of measuring elevation showed that its prior elevations were up to two feet lower than it had thought.

Due to subsidence over the years, walls and levees that were supposed to be 14 feet above sea level might only be 12 feet. But the engineer in charge told his staff to continue using the old measurement system because that was the one in use in 1965, when the project was authorized by Congress.

The corps' 2008 internal review of the storm protection system noted that the agency continued to report that the project would protect against the Standard

Project Hurricane—the 200-year storm—"even though the datum error and benchmark decision made that unlikely."

Critics have long been frustrated by the corps' habit of blindly following Congress' initial orders rather than lobbying for improvements to deal with new information. It's true, Davis said, that the corps can only act when Congress passes a law and funds the job. But he argued that the agency has the leeway to adapt to changing circumstances.

In fact, in 1965 the first corps' first project directors increased the design specifications of the hurricane protection system based on Hurricane Betsy, which showed that storm surge could be higher than expected. The authorization, wrote a corps official, "is broad enough to allow reconsideration of the degree of protection."

But fellow corps employees, as well as the agency's 2008 review, said later that they were under pressure to

In May 2006 construction workers put the finishing touches on a rebuilt section of a levee that had been breached in the aftermath of Hurricane Katrina. (© Mario Tama/ Getty Images.)

keep costs down and finish projects on time. So they didn't strengthen the system.

Even today, corps officials point to that 1965 legislation as a constraint.

Ken Holder, chief of public affairs of the corps' New Orleans district, said the original system could be built only to "reduce the damage from a specifically selected 'Design Hurricane' with the specific characteristics" outlined in the law.

The Revised Strategy for the Corps of Engineers After Katrina

As Congress began looking at rebuilding the system after Katrina, the Standard Project Hurricane gained renewed attention.

Considering that Katrina—a Category 3 storm—had destroyed the old system, the city and state pushed for Category 5 protection. But the [President] George W. Bush administration—and some members of Congress—didn't like the costs.

> [New Orleans' flood protection] system . . . would now be replaced by one that only had to be good enough to secure flood insurance.

Barely two months after the disaster, the president's head of the rebuilding effort, Donald Powell, put the Category 5 idea to rest, saying, "The commitment is to build the levees back to a 3 . . . and then to study the 5."

But when Congress authorized the rebuilding of the system two years later in the 2007 Water Resources Development Act, it didn't mention hurricane intensity or the Standard Project Hurricane.

Instead the corps was told to raise walls and levees to the level of protection necessary to participate in the National Flood Insurance Program.

A system that once was supposed to defeat the "most severe meteorological conditions" would now be replaced by one that only had to be good enough to secure flood insurance—protection from a so-called 100-year flood. (A 100-year flood is a storm that has a 1 percent chance of happening in any year, not a storm that occurs once a century.)

Political leaders and others involved in the post-Katrina negotiations say there were two major drivers for the sudden change: money and the urgent need to regain flood insurance.

"It was always about money with the Bush people," recalled Kathleen Blanco, Louisiana's governor at the time. "Everyone remembers when the president came down and said he was going to make it right, build it back better and stronger. And I think he really meant that.

"But then when the corps started putting the numbers together, the administration was just not going to go there."

Sen. Mary Landrieu, D-La., was one of the leading voices at the time for Category 5 protection. Her staff declined repeated requests for an interview, instead providing *The Lens* with a statement that didn't address our questions.

Davis, who was involved in post-storm planning as the head of the Coalition to Restore Coastal Louisiana, said getting insurance quickly was paramount.

"There could be no rebuilding or attracting and keeping businesses without flood insurance," he said. "There was an urgency, almost a panic, over the issue." Building to the lower standard was not only cheaper, but faster.

The New System Is Still Better than the Old One

Local corps officials say the current 100-year system is built to more demanding specifications than those laid out [in] 1965 for a 200- or 300-year storm.

Critics agree, but say those improvements don't measure up to what science now knows would be the "most severe conditions" that can reasonably be expected in this region—storms worse than Katrina.

Bob Jacobsen, an engineer who completed an in-depth evaluation of the new system for the local Flood Protection Authority, said there's "no question" the new system is a lower standard of protection than that 1965 charge demanded.

"Now, is what they built a good system, better than what it replaced? Yes, no question," he said. "But is it adequate? No, not given what's at risk here.

"And does it meet that original standard ordered in 1965? No."

How much higher would the flood protection system need to be to protect against the "most severe storm"? Engineers say it's hard to quantify.

The heights of levees and floodwalls ringing the metro area are not uniform because computer models have shown storm surge levels would be different at each location.

> 'It's a standard that's been set for obtaining affordable flood insurance only.'

For example, some sections of levee along Lakeshore Drive are 16 feet above sea level; others along the Gulf Intracoastal Waterway are 21.5 feet.

With that variability in mind, Jacobsen estimated 500-year protection would require an additional 1 to 2 feet along the entire system, without accounting for the added height of wind-driven waves.

"If you add in wave conditions, in some areas you might be talking about needing 3 to 4 feet higher," Jacobsen said.

The switch to the flood-insurance standard has had another, equally troubling effect, critics said, because a system designed to protect people would be more robust than one built to save property.

"In effect, it's not really a standard that's been set for safety reasons, it's a standard that's been set for obtaining affordable flood insurance only," said Bob Turner, an engineer who is the regional director of the Southeast Louisiana Flood Protection Authority–East.

"The system should be based on protecting what's at risk, and in a highly populated urban area, that is something much greater than the cost of property damage," Turner stressed.

The Current System Can Be Strengthened

The corps and the Flood Protection Authority say the current system can be brought to what is considered a "resiliency level" of 500-year protection—meaning the walls and levees would stand up even if they were overtopped by something stronger than a 100-year storm.

This could be done by armoring—with grass or synthetic mats—the side of earthen levees facing the city.

But Rick Luettich, a noted storm surge modeler and a member of the local Flood Protection Authority board, said this isn't the same as building the system New Orleans needs. A 100-year system with resilience added does not provide the same level of confidence as a system built to a 500-year standard, he said.

> As sea levels rise and the city becomes more exposed, people will not want to move to New Orleans.

"It's sort of back-engineering," he said. "Up-front it should have a much higher design standard applied to it. And in the long run that's what you want for this area. I've always said that, and I still believe that."

Leuttich and Turner also point to research that shows the onset of global warming is likely to result in more large storms.

A recent review of the new hurricane protection system raised many of the same criticisms, including an overemphasis on protecting property, not people.

Geographer Ezra Boyd of DisasterMap.net coordinated the report. He pointed to a study by noted Dutch engineers who said the life and property at risk in New Orleans warrant 1,000- to 4,000-year protection.

The Dutch system, in contrast, uses a standard of 10,000 years in vulnerable areas—100 times more robust than the one nearing completion around New Orleans.

Local corps officials said even if they had the freedom to strengthen the levee system, their 2007 marching orders superseded the 1965 instructions. And while that authorization remains open, they said, Congress would have to provide new orders and funding.

Davis said the corps' argument "might be right in a law-school debating sense" but it misses the intent of Congress in 1965, and that law remains on the books.

He contends the city should take its case to court to argue that Congress has not lived up to the 1965 standard. The 2007 orders "were a detour, not a redirection," he argued.

As sea levels rise and the city becomes more exposed, people will not want to move to New Orleans, Davis said.

"A major metro area that has only a razor-thin commitment with insurability is one that is gambling with its future," he said. "In 1965 Congress said we needed and deserved a level of protection to meet those risks. We still do today."

The Response to Hurricane Katrina Demonstrated Americans' Resilience

Barack Obama

In the following viewpoint, President Barack Obama reflects upon the fifth anniversary of Hurricane Katrina. In the wake of disaster, the president says that New Orleans has become a symbol of resilience. He chronicles the dedication of those involved in the relief effort. There is still a lot of work to be done, the president says, and many residents who have returned to the area are still struggling. He vows that his administration will continue to support the recovery effort in the Gulf Coast and work to prepare for future threats to prevent another catastrophe like Katrina. Obama is the forty-fourth president of the United States.

SOURCE. Barack Obama, "Remarks by the President on the Fifth Anniversary of Hurricane Katrina in New Orleans, Louisiana," August 29, 2010. www.whitehouse.gov. Public Domain.

It's been five years [2010] since Katrina ravaged the Gulf Coast. There's no need to dwell on what you experienced and what the world witnessed. We all remember it keenly: water pouring through broken levees; mothers holding their children above the waterline; people stranded on rooftops begging for help; bodies lying in the streets of a great American city. It was a natural disaster but also a manmade catastrophe—a shameful breakdown in government that left countless men, and women, and children abandoned and alone.

And shortly after the storm, I came down to Houston to spend time with some of the folks who had taken shelter there. And I'll never forget what one woman told me. She said, "We had nothing before the hurricane. And now we've got less than nothing."

In the years that followed, New Orleans could have remained a symbol of destruction and decay; of a storm that came and the inadequate response that followed. It was not hard to imagine a day when we'd tell our children that a once vibrant and wonderful city had been laid low by indifference and neglect. But that's not what happened. It's not what happened at Ben Franklin [High School]. It's not what happened here at Xavier [University]. It's not what happened across New Orleans and across the Gulf Coast. Instead this city has become a symbol of resilience and of community and of the fundamental responsibility that we have to one another.

> This city has become a symbol of resilience and of community and of the fundamental responsibility that we have to one another.

And we see that here at Xavier. Less than a month after the storm struck, amidst debris and flood-damaged buildings, President [Norman] Francis promised that this university would reopen in a matter of months. Some said he was crazy. Some said it couldn't happen. But they didn't count on what happens when one force of nature meets another. And by January [2006]—four months later—class was in session. Less than a year after the storm, I had the privilege of delivering a commencement address to the largest graduating class in Xavier's history. That is a symbol of what New Orleans is all about.

We see New Orleans in the efforts of Joycelyn Heintz, who's here today. Katrina left her house 14 feet underwater. But after volunteers helped her rebuild, she joined AmeriCorps to serve the community herself—part of a wave of AmeriCorps members who've been critical to the rebirth of this city and the rebuilding of this region. So today, she manages a local center for mental health and wellness.

We see the symbol that this city has become in the St. Bernard Project, whose founder Liz McCartney is with us. This endeavor has drawn volunteers from across the country to rebuild hundreds of homes throughout St. Bernard Parish and the Lower Ninth Ward.

Dedication to the Community

I've seen the sense of purpose people felt after the storm when I visited Musicians' Village in the Ninth Ward back in 2006. Volunteers were not only constructing houses; they were coming together to preserve the culture of music and art that's part of the soul of this city—and the soul of this country. And today, more than 70 homes are complete, and construction is underway on the Ellis Marsalis Center for Music.

We see the dedication to the community in the efforts of Xavier grad Dr. Regina Benjamin, who mortgaged her home, maxed out her credit cards so she could reopen her Bayou la Batre clinic to care for victims of the storm—and who is now our nation's Surgeon General.

And we see resilience and hope exemplified by students at Carver High School, who have helped to raise more than a million dollars to build a new community track and football field—their "Field of Dreams"—for the Ninth Ward.

So because of all of you—all the advocates, all the organizers who are here today, folks standing behind me who've worked so hard, who never gave up hope—you are all leading the way toward a better future for this city with innovative approaches to fight poverty and improve health care, reduce crime, and create opportunities for young people. Because of you, New Orleans is coming back.

And I just came from Parkway Bakery and Tavern. Five years ago, the storm nearly destroyed that neighborhood institution. I saw the pictures. Now they're open, business is booming, and that's some good eats. I had the shrimp po'boy and some of the gumbo. But I skipped the bread pudding because I thought I might fall asleep while I was speaking. But I've got it saved for later.

> My administration is going to stand with you—and fight alongside you—until the job is done.

Five years ago, many questioned whether people could ever return to this city. Today, New Orleans is one of the fastest growing cities in America, with a big new surge in small businesses. Five years ago, the Saints had to play every game on the road because of the damage to the Superdome. Two weeks ago, we welcomed the Saints to the White House as Super Bowl champions. There was also food associated with that. We marked the occasion with a 30-foot po'boy made with shrimps and oysters from the Gulf. And you'll be pleased to know there were no leftovers.

Now, I don't have to tell you that there are still too many vacant and overgrown lots. There are still too many students attending classes in trailers. There are still too many people unable to find work. And there are still too many New Orleanians, folks who haven't been able to come home. So while an incredible amount of progress has been made, on this fifth anniversary, I wanted to come here and tell the people of this city directly: My administration is going to stand with you—and fight alongside you—until the job is done. Until New Orleans is all the way back, all the way.

The Commitment to Katrina Recovery

When I took office, I directed my Cabinet to redouble our efforts, to put an end to the turf wars between agencies, to cut the red tape and cut the bureaucracy. I wanted to make sure that the federal government was a partner—not an obstacle—to recovery here in the Gulf Coast. And members of my Cabinet—including EPA [US Environmental Protection Agency] administrator, Lisa Jackson, who grew up in Pontchartrain Park—they have come down here dozens of times. [Secretary of Housing and Urban Development] Shaun Donovan has come down here dozens of times. This is not just to make appearances. It's not just to get photo ops. They came down here to listen and to learn and make real the changes that were necessary so that government was actually working for you.

So for example, efforts to rebuild schools and hospitals, to repair damaged roads and bridges, to get people back to their homes—they were tied up for years in a tangle of disagreements and byzantine rules. So when I took office, working with your outstanding delegation, particularly Senator Mary Landrieu, we put in place a new way of resolving disputes. We put in place a new way of resolving disputes so that funds set aside for rebuilding efforts actually went toward rebuilding efforts. And as a result, more than 170 projects are getting underway—work on firehouses, and police stations, and roads, and sewer systems, and health clinics, and libraries, and universities.

We're tackling the corruption and inefficiency that has long plagued the New Orleans Housing Authority. We're helping homeowners rebuild and making it easier

New Orleans Is the First All-Charter School District

As a result of Hurricane Katrina and consistently low academic performance, public education in New Orleans has redeveloped under a decentralized governance model. In 2005, the state Board of Elementary and Secondary Education (BESE) placed the majority of public schools under the oversight of the Recovery School District (RSD). The local Orleans Parish School Board (OPSB) retained control and oversight of 17 schools. As families returned to the city, charter schools began to dominate the portfolio of public schools serving students in the city. . . . At its peak, RSD operated 35 direct-run schools. When the 2013–14 school year ended, RSD closed its last five remaining direct-run schools, making RSD-New Orleans the first 100 percent urban charter school district.

SOURCE. *Patrick Sims and Debra Vaughan, "The State of Public Education in New Orleans: 2014 Report," Tulane University Cowen Institute for Public Education Initiatives, pp. 2, 8. www.speno2014.com/wp-content/uploads/2014/08/SPENO-HQ.pdf.*

for renters to find affordable options. And we're helping people to move out of temporary homes. You know, when I took office, more than three years after the storm, tens of thousands of families were still stuck in disaster housing—many still living in small trailers that had been provided by FEMA [Federal Emergency Management Agency]. We were spending huge sums of money on temporary shelters when we knew it would be better for families, and less costly for taxpayers, to help people get into affordable, stable, and more permanent housing. So we've helped make it possible for people to find those homes, and we've dramatically reduced the number of families in emergency housing.

On the health care front, as a candidate for President, I pledged to make sure we were helping New Orleans recruit doctors and nurses, and rebuild medical facilities—including a new veterans hospital. Well, we have resolved a long-standing dispute—one that had tied up hundreds of millions of dollars—to fund the replacement for Charity Hospital. And in June [2010], Veterans Secretary Ric Shinseki came to New Orleans for the groundbreaking of that new VA hospital.

In education, we've made strides as well. As you know, schools in New Orleans were falling behind long before Katrina. But in the years since the storm, a lot of public schools opened themselves up to innovation and to reform. And as a result, we're actually seeing rising achievement, and New Orleans is becoming a model of innovation for the nation. This is yet another sign that

> We're also focusing on preparing for future threats so that there is never another disaster like Katrina.

you're not just rebuilding—you're rebuilding stronger than before. Just this Friday [August 27, 2010], my administration announced a final agreement on $1.8 billion dollars for Orleans Parish schools. This is money that had been locked up for years, but now it's freed up so folks here can determine best how to restore the school system.

And in a city that's known too much violence, that's seen too many young people lost to drugs and criminal activity, we've got a Justice Department that's committed to working with New Orleans to fight the scourge of violent crime, and to weed out corruption in the police force, and to ensure the criminal justice system works for everyone in this city. And I want everybody to hear—to know and to hear me thank Mitch Landrieu, your new mayor, for his commitment to that partnership.

Preparing for the Future

Now, even as we continue our recovery efforts, we're also focusing on preparing for future threats so that there is never another disaster like Katrina. The largest civil works project in American history is underway to build a fortified levee system. And as I—just as I pledged as a candidate, we're going to finish this system by next year so that this city is protected against a 100-year storm. We should not be playing Russian roulette every hurricane season. And we're also working to restore protective wetlands and natural barriers that were not only damaged by Katrina—were not just damaged by Katrina but had been rapidly disappearing for decades.

In Washington, we are restoring competence and accountability. I am proud that my FEMA Director, Craig Fugate, has 25 years of experience in disaster management in Florida. He came from Florida, a state that has known its share of hurricanes. We've put together a group led by Secretary Donovan and Secretary [of Homeland Security Janet] Napolitano to look at disaster recovery across the country. We're improving coordination on the ground, and modernizing emergency communications, helping families plan for a crisis. And we're putting in place reforms so that never again in America is somebody left behind in a disaster because they're living with a disability or because they're elderly or because they're infirmed. That will not happen again.

Finally, even as you've been buffeted by Katrina and Rita, even as you've been impacted by the broader recession that has devastated communities across the country, in recent months the Gulf Coast has seen new hardship as a result of the BP Deepwater Horizon oil spill. And just as we've sought to ensure that we are doing what it takes to recover from Katrina, my administration has worked hard to match our efforts on the spill to what you need on the ground. And we've been in close consultation with your governor, your mayors, your parish presidents, your local government officials.

And from the start, I promised you two things. One is that we would see to it that the leak was stopped. And it has been. The second promise I made was that we would stick with our efforts, and stay on BP, until the damage to the Gulf and to the lives of the people in this region was reversed. And this, too, is a promise that we will keep. We are not going to forget. We're going to stay on it until this area is fully recovered.

That's why we rapidly launched the largest response to an environmental disaster in American history—47,000 people on the ground, 5,700 vessels on the water—to contain and clean up the oil. When BP was not moving fast enough on claims, we told BP to set aside $20 billion in a fund—managed by an independent third party—to help all those whose lives have been turned upside down by the spill.

> Thanks to the great people of this great city, New Orleans is blossoming again.

And we will continue to rely on sound science, carefully monitoring waters and coastlines as well as the health of the people along the Gulf, to deal with any long-term effects of the oil spill. We are going to stand with you until the oil is cleaned up, until the environment is restored, until polluters are held accountable, until communities are made whole, and until this region is all the way back on its feet.

So that's how we're helping this city, and this state, and this region to recover from the worst natural disaster in our nation's history. We're cutting through the red tape that has impeded rebuilding efforts for years. We're making government work better and smarter, in coordination with one of the most expansive non-profit efforts in American history. We're helping state and local leaders to address serious problems that had been neglected for decades—problems that existed before the storm came, and have continued after the waters receded—from the levee system to the justice system, from the health care system to the education system.

Hurricane Katrina's Ultimate Legacy

And together, we are helping to make New Orleans a place that stands for what we can do in America—not just for what we can't do. Ultimately, that must be the legacy of Katrina: not one of neglect, but of action; not one of indifference, but of empathy; not of abandonment, but of a community working together to meet shared challenges.

The truth is, there are some wounds that have not yet healed. And there are some losses that can't be repaid. And for many who lived through those harrowing days five years ago, there's searing memories that time may not erase. But even amid so much tragedy, we saw stirrings of a brighter day. Five years ago we saw men and women risking their own safety to save strangers. We saw nurses staying behind to care for the sick and the injured. We saw families coming home to clean up and rebuild—not just their own homes, but their neighbors' homes, as well. And we saw music and Mardi Gras and the vibrancy, the fun of this town undiminished. And we've seen many return to their beloved city with a newfound sense of appreciation and obligation to this community.

And when I came here four years ago, one thing I found striking was all the greenery that had begun to come back. And I was reminded of a passage from the book of Job. "There is hope for a tree if it be cut down that it will sprout again, and that its tender branch will not cease." The work ahead will not be easy, and there will be setbacks. There will be challenges along the way. But thanks to you, thanks to the great people of this great city, New Orleans is blossoming again.

CHAPTER 3

Personal Narratives

A Journalist Reflects About Covering Hurricane Katrina

Penny Owen

In the following viewpoint, a journalist reflects upon covering the aftermath of Hurricane Katrina. She spent a week in the outlying areas of New Orleans talking to residents who were able to evacuate the city. It was heartbreaking to talk to evacuees about their harrowing escape from the New Orleans floodwaters, the author reflects. As the days went by, people suffered horrific conditions, and the author no longer recognized her own country. Penny Owen (formerly Cockerell) is a reporter for the Associated Press and a former staff reporter for the *Daily Oklahoman* in Oklahoma City.

I arrived on Monday afternoon [August 29, 2005] and spent about a week covering the aftermath of Hurricane Katrina in the outlying areas of New Orleans.

SOURCE. Penny Owen, "Words Fail," Dart Center for Journalism and Trauma, September 2, 2005. Copyright © 2005 Penny Owen. All rights reserved. Reproduced with permission.

First it was just frustrating. There was no Internet access, calls weren't getting through, and official knowledge was sketchy at best. My main concerns, as I drove south from Dallas, were transmitting a story on deadline and chasing Oklahomans responding to needs in the Gulf Coast area.

Conditions Go from Bad to Horrible

Then it became heartbreaking. The first refugees I met in the aftermath of Hurricane Katrina—those who got out and arrived in the outlying areas of New Orleans—talked of damaged homes, and businesses they may never see again. Some left behind pets, photos, belongings they could never replace.

Then it got worse.

Hour by hour, more refugees came out of New Orleans, plucked from rooftops, some having waded through a "toxic soup" for rescue—a lucky few were lifted to safety, while thousands were left behind. Many were rescued by civilians in flat-bottom boats passing by. They showed up at shelters in Baton Rouge and elsewhere with nothing but what they wore. I had to wonder how they got out infants and wheelchair-bound relatives, but some did. And they were all so desperate, begging for help, it was hard not to be drawn in.

> Life, as I knew it, was suspended.

Then it became surreal. Life, as I knew it, was suspended. My lifeline to normalcy was my editor, Sonya Colberg, who provided good, rational advice in the midst of an unraveling situation. And yet I knew I wasn't even seeing the worst of it, just down the road on Interstate 10. I was safe—but what about my colleagues, like Natalie Pompilio of the *Philadelphia Inquirer*, who arrived in New Orleans before the storm?

I both envied those "inside" for their access and worried about their safety. Should I dare to reach New

Water-damaged hallways in New Orleans's Memorial Medical Center sit empty on September 11, 2005, after the facility was evacuated. Conditions inside the hospital—like elsewhere in the city—quickly deteriorated to untenable levels in the aftermath of Hurricane Katrina. (© Dina Rudick/The Boston Globe via Getty Images.)

Orleans, or just cover the mess out here? My head swirled. But there was plenty to go around.

At the Baton Rouge River Center, Arthur D. Smith told me of his harrowing escape to his own rooftop, where he contemplated death as he stretched his numb feet into gutters to heave himself up. "I thought, 'God, I don't want to die like this,'" he said.

The 77-year-old diabetic spent two days waiting in the scorching sun for rescue. He stood wet, smelly and relieved in a line for newly arrived refugees.

After the interview, Smith asked me to call his family and rattled off a number. I called after deadline, got through eventually, and asked the man who answered if he knew "Arthur." "Jesus," the man said. I thought he was dead. I told him where to find Arthur, hung up, and cried.

Each day brought concern from state and federal officials. They realized the "frustration" and "were addressing it." But it wasn't frustrating any longer, it was a "desperate SOS," as New Orleans Mayor Ray Nagin put it. People weren't just hungry or angry, but dying. Hospitals had run out of generator juice. The normal "honeymoon" that typically follows a tragedy never came. It just went from worse to horrible.

> The normal 'honeymoon' that typically follows a tragedy never came. It just went from worse to horrible.

I started feeling guilty about having a hotel room in a hotel that had opened their conference rooms for refugees to sleep on the floor. I recognized the feeling of inadequacy in finding stories to define the scope of this catastrophe, and in finding the words once I found a story. We dilute words—everything is horrible and disastrous, or heroic and so on. Where are the words that raise the bar to this?

The Situation Spirals Out of Control

Each day brought something more jarring than the last. When New Orleans Mayor Ray Nagin began cussing and crying on a local radio station, it was, frankly, shocking. Could it really be that out of control? And who was in charge?

By Thursday [September 1, 2005], all bets were off. People were angry. Reporters were angry, and I was angry too. As an Oklahoman who covered numerous tornadoes and the Oklahoma City bombing, I understand tragedy, especially a natural disaster, but a response this slow was frightening and surreal. I went in search of the Louisiana National Guard and found them—I called their headquarters, but could not find anyone who knew anything or who had time to talk, so I had to show up to talk. They, too, had little communication in their small headquarters at an airport in Hammond, just north of

New Orleans. Help from other states was coming, but Master Sgt. Bruce Stein of the 236th Air National Guard Combat Communications Squadron couldn't say from where, nor could he say where they were going or for how long. This was not because he was withholding information, but because he really didn't know. But he did know this:

"You know what they're saying on the news," Stein said. "It's worse than that."

Helicopters and C-130 cargo planes would land and take off from this small municipal airport, but what happened in between would not be communicated because, as one guardsman said, troops didn't have a way to communicate with other state troops. Soon, my little frustrations with filing a story or finding a meal paled in comparison to what these people were going through. At least I had a car, and gas, and a home to go back to. I filed my stories via dictation and, when I got lucky, by e-mail. Then I drove for miles for the next story because phone lines were still down and the only way to find out what was going on was, again, to show up.

At the hotel I stayed in, and elsewhere, locals talked about the bad segment of New Orleans, saying their worst kind were those stuck in that city. Some stayed because they chose not to leave, but others said they couldn't leave because they couldn't pay $30 for a bus ticket, were too ill, too old, had pets, or just underestimated Hurricane Katrina. Second-guessing will go on for months and it starts with the evacuation. Why no public transportation? Why no stronger force?

> I no longer recognized my own country—not in Louisiana, where people who survived were reduced to animal-like conditions.

Katrina Leaves Behind a Changed Country

And then it became mind-boggling. Words fail when Americans die in lawn chairs and are left to rot in the sun. When hospitals are looted and corpses are laid in stairwells because the basement morgue is flooded.

I no longer had problems. And I no longer recognized my own country—not in Louisiana, where people who survived were reduced to animal-like conditions for indefinite periods of time.

But leaving the area left me with mixed feelings. I didn't want to let go of writing about this catastrophe—a true catastrophe. My fear is that we'll forget New Orleans and the Gulf Coast way too soon, that attention spans will wane and media reports will dim. This hurricane will change our country's landscape and the repercussions will be felt nationwide. Bad as it is, that is a good thing, because until Americans feel a personal pinch, too many will forget the horror, even when it happens so close to home.

The Former FEMA Director Recalls His Leadership During Hurricane Katrina

Michael D. Brown and Ted Schwarz

In the following viewpoint, the former director of the Federal Emergency Management Agency (FEMA) reflects upon his experience during Hurricane Katrina. He writes about the days leading up to the storm, when the National Hurricane Center predicted that the levees in New Orleans were likely to fail. He relates his initial conversation with state and local officials in Louisiana, as well as his concerns about the lack of resources available in the area. In the aftermath of the storm, he became the face of the government's ineffectual response to the catastrophe. Michael D. Brown was the director of FEMA from January 2003 to September 2005. Ted Schwarz is a writer who has authored or coauthored more than one hundred books.

SOURCE. Michael D. Brown and Ted Schwarz, *Deadly Indifference: The Perfect (Political) Storm: Hurricane Katrina, The Bush White House, and Beyond.* Boulder, CO: Taylor Trade Publishing, 2011.

In August 2005 I became the third most powerful person in the country confronting the impending disaster of Hurricane Katrina, a storm that would take hundreds of lives and destroy most of one of the great cities in the nation.

Katrina was not unexpected. The storm had been building in intensity, gradually approaching the Florida Keys and the Gulf of Mexico with all the force of a military assault. Dozens of federal and state agencies were on high alert and ready to supply whatever relief would be needed as the storm passed through each of their regions, having started their monitoring and planning while the soon-to-be-hurricane was still a tropical storm in the Atlantic. The movement of rescue workers and supplies—food, water, shelter, medical care, financial assistance—would be swift and adaptable because hurricanes have minds of their own. They are like bulls in a rodeo ring, seemingly aiming in one direction then shifting here and there as though on an impulsive, self-directed sightseeing tour. This was the problem, though I did not realize it at the time: exactly how that uncertainty was affecting politicians' decisions in the regions where the hurricane might strike.

The random nature of hurricanes was something I understood. In the past we might see a hurricane traveling with such force that it was certain to flatten a Florida coastal community, for example, only to have it veer off by a hundred miles. The city that had been expected to bear the brunt of the storm had homes boarded and the occupants evacuated. The community caught by surprise had inadequately prepared residents. The community we thought would need disaster relief had only disgruntled citizens complaining that they were forced to evacuate for nothing. The community caught in the unexpected hurricane shift had residents who lost pets, possessions, or family members. The survivors were angry, certain they had been betrayed by the "experts," unable to grasp the vagaries of a storm's movement, and often wreaking political vengeance by voting out their local government leaders. Such problems could not be avoided. However, the aftermath served as a warning to politicians—mayors, city managers, and governors—facing similar decisions with future storms. React before you know what you are reacting against and constituents will be outraged if you're wrong. React when you are certain of what you are acting against and you may be too late. This was certainly the problem with Louisiana and its most famous city, New Orleans.

> Hurricane Katrina was our major concern at the end of August and early part of September 2005.

Coordinating the Response Effort

Hurricane Katrina was our major concern at the end of August and early part of September 2005. On August 29, 2005, nineteen hours before Hurricane Katrina slammed into the shore along the Louisiana coast, I was briefing President [George W.] Bush, Homeland Security Chief (my boss) Michael Chertoff, and local officials on the readiness plans. Max Mayfield, the director of the National Hurricane Center, explained the severity of the hurricane and the fact that the storm covered a much wider area than had been seen in the past. He was certain that there was a good chance the levees would be breached, an action that would flood New Orleans. Anyone with any experience in natural disasters knows those classic disasters we all discuss and anticipate. New Orleans was one of those. Below sea level, we always knew New Orleans could turn into a fishbowl if the levees failed. Now, here was my good friend and fellow Oklahoman, Max Mayfield, director of the National Hurricane Center, telling the governor of Louisiana and the mayor of New Orleans that the theory could easily turn into the reality.

Michael Brown (right), then-director of the Federal Emergency Management Agency, briefs President George W. Bush about damage caused by Hurricane Katrina on September 2, 2005. (© AP Images/ Susan Walsh.)

I explained that Mayor Ray Nagin and his staff had settled on their Superdome stadium as the place of last refuge. I said that the choice was highly questionable. The Superdome was twelve feet below water level, protected only if the levees held, and the roof did not seem structurally sound enough to withstand the storm. In addition, because there had been no evacuation, conditions were likely to overwhelm available state and local rescue personnel. I explained that I was certain this was likely to be the big national disaster for which we had trained, and I was concerned that there were not enough supplies and personnel in position to safely ride out the storm, then immediately move in to effect search and rescue.

The President Ignored the Warning

President Bush said nothing during the closed-circuit videoconference. He had no questions, expressed no concerns. However, after the storm hit, when there was criticism of problems that should have been avoided, he immediately went into CYA [cover your ass] mode. Four days following his participation in the videoconference while at his ranch in Crawford, Texas, he told the Associated Press, "There is frustration but I want people to know that help's coming. I don't think that anybody anticipated the breach of the levees."

The President came through, rightly so, as a man who cared, who was concerned that the government do everything possible after being surprised by the intensity of the storm. In truth, it seemed to me that either he did not pay any attention to Mayfield's warning or he lied. These two possibilities became known only when the Associated Press obtained a copy of the videoconference and aired it nationally—six months after the fact. By then I was no longer part of the government.

> Had I not been a scapegoat, someone else would have been.

Had I not been a scapegoat, someone else would have been. The reality of government, any government, is that when leadership morphs into deadly indifference . . . there are those who will do anything to keep their jobs. They fear that often what is best for the people they were elected or appointed to serve may not be in their own best interest, and NIMBI [Not in My Best Interest] becomes the de facto consideration for both planning and response. . . .

The Political Aftermath

Looking back at Katrina's damage to New Orleans I realize that what I encountered was the perfect political storm. There was driving wind reaching well over 100 miles per hour. There was pouring rain blown by the wind; it went from a downfall to a wall of water surging against houses and high-rises. And there was the most coveted award awaiting those local politicians who had the tenacity to seek high ground before the storm hit, then fight the immediate aftermath with the ultimate weapons at their disposal—spontaneous press conferences, photo opportunities, and what could have been the wisdom of hindsight if they had started with any awareness at all.

By now you may be thinking to yourself that this is going to be a . . . condemnation of one political party or another. You may even remember the ultimate kiss of death for any high-level presidential appointee, the President's praise in the midst of disaster, and think this is a partisan [viewpoint]. You're wrong. The problems FEMA [Federal Emergency Management Agency] and the Department of Homeland Security encountered will occur again and again; natural disasters are no respecter of political parties, politicians' egos, or anything else, and those same politicians will fail to deal with uncomfortable realities they cannot prevent.

Volunteer Services for Katrina Victims: A Personal Story

Carolyn Duff

In the following viewpoint, a volunteer reflects on helping the victims of Hurricane Katrina after they arrived at the Houston Astrodome. There were numerous Houston-area residents who opened their homes to Katrina evacuees, the author says. In addition there were frequent announcements inside the Astrodome of departing buses to cities outside of Houston that were offering free transportation, financial assistance, and job placement. Many people wanted to help the victims of the storm, the author says—so many, in fact, that the Astrodome had to turn volunteers away at times. Carolyn Duff is a program manager at the University of Texas MD Anderson Cancer Center.

SOURCE. Carolyn Duff, "Volunteer Services for Katrina Victims: A Personal Story," *Internet Journal of Rescue and Disaster Medicine,* vol. 5, no. 2, 2005. Copyright © 2005 Internet Scientific Publications LLC. All rights reserved. Reproduced with permission.

Saturday morning, September 3 [2005], a Red Cross representative needed someone to walk around the Astrodome making a record of where things were so that volunteers could have a resource to answer questions from evacuees. I took on this job and went through all the levels of the Dome, noting the location of restroom facilities, men's and women's showers, food, snacks, medical triage and pharmaceutical dispensary, lost & found people, clothing distribution, baby needs, the FEMA and Social Security on-site headquarters, the phone bank (SBC is donating $4 million per month for free long distance to help reunite displaced families), and the computer room where evacuees could access the internet for 30-minute intervals and post their names to missing-person web sites, or check those sites to see if their loved ones had posted a message. One New Orleans resident was especially anxious to use the computer. The only information she had about her mother was that she had gone to Baton Rouge to stay with relatives. She said, "I didn't even know we had relatives in Baton Rouge!"

Breakfast was being served from tables lined up around the 4th floor of the Astrodome. There were enough donuts, bagels, muffins and cereal to feed four times the number of evacuees. Cots were lined up not just on the Dome floor but around the outer perimeter on all levels. Many cots had signs posted above them listing the names of missing loved ones. It was early in the morning when I arrived and many of Houston's newest residents were still asleep, no small feat considering the frequency of announcements over the PA system.

Saturday evening I helped with clothing distribution. Boxes of clothing were arriving in a steady stream, most needing to be sorted. There were several volunteers working to organize clothing. Many of the donated boxes contained winter clothing. Someone had a pair of scissors and was cutting off the arms of long-sleeve garments. We were working at a feverish pace to finish sorting because at 8:00 PM, other volunteers were scheduled to begin taking orders for clothing items needed. After taking the order, a runner would go to the distribution area, fill the order, then take it back to the one who placed the order. I was in charge of several large boxes of brand-new ladies' underwear, still in the package. As fast as I could open the packages, I was giving away the contents. At times there were 5–6 runners at once shouting for different sizes. For the next two hours, clothing orders were filled and distributed at breakneck speed. In spite of the chaos, the operation ran smoothly. Unfortunately, I ran out of the smaller size panties, and then even the medium and large size underwear ran out. At 10:00 PM the Red Cross rep stopped the operation so the volunteers could take a break, reorganize their boxes, and begin the operation again at 10:30. I called it a night since I didn't have anything left to give away but a few packages of XXL ladies' underwear.

> It didn't take long to discover that . . . they really didn't need any [more] volunteers.

Sunday afternoon, September 4, there was a sign posted outside the Dome saying, "No volunteers needed until 6:00 PM." I had seen the same sign the day before but this time I ignored it and went on in. I was wearing my wristband from the day before and had no problem gaining admission. It didn't take long to discover that the sign was correct, they really didn't need any volunteers. There were plenty of people sorting the new boxes of clothing that had come in, and there was no other apparent way to make myself useful. I waited at the staging area and talked with a young woman whose job it was to place hurricane victims with local residents offering their homes. She was elated to report that she had just placed a family of 14 with a man from California. The man had flown to Houston on his Lear jet with his teenage daughter to find a family they could help. She told me many stories of generous Houston-area residents who had opened their hearts and doors to Katrina refugees. Even while we were talking, a couple from Katy introduced themselves to her and offered rooms in their home. Another man from Austin had flown in earlier that day and set up an evacuated family in one of his vacant properties, bought them a used car, and arranged for job placement. The woman who was helping to make these connections had just been laid off and was going to have to begin looking for a job herself. In spite of her own hardship, she saw the layoff as a blessing, realizing there was no way she could have devoted as much time to this effort as she could have if she'd still been employed.

> All the evacuees I encountered expressed how grateful they were for the help they were receiving.

Over the PA system, there were frequent announcements that buses would be leaving for destinations including San Antonio, Austin, even Minnesota. The departure times were announced and anyone who wanted to go to that city was welcome to board that bus. With each announcement came the promise of financial assistance, job placement, and free bus transportation to the destination.

A young woman who had just arrived at the Dome asked where she could find a cot. After being processed as an evacuee, she wasn't told where she should sleep. By that time, several people had been relocated to other cities or reunited with their family members, and there were a number of empty cots both on the floor and in the hallways of the outer perimeter. After giving her direction on where to bunk, she asked where to find the medical triage area. She had been separated from her mother and other family members so she hitchhiked from Louisiana. En route to Houston she was raped. She hadn't told her mother because she didn't want her to worry. As we talked her eyes filled with tears and she said she couldn't think about her ordeal anymore because it was all so overwhelming.

All the evacuees I encountered expressed how grateful they were for the help they were receiving. At every opportunity I welcomed these new neighbors to Houston and told them how glad we are they're here.

As I waited for an assignment, I noticed a single mother who was obviously distressed. She was scheduled to go to the FEMA office on the 4th floor and didn't have anyone to watch her children, twin fourth-grade girls and a two-year-old boy. Children were not allowed on the 4th floor (I'm not sure whether they weren't allowed up there at all or just in the FEMA office). There was a daycare center on the ground level but they wouldn't take children under age four. Everyone she asked for help referred her to someone else and she was getting desperate. I was standing nearby so I offered to watch her children

Volunteers at the Astrodome in Houston, Texas, sort thousands of shoes donated for Hurricane Katrina victims on September 3, 2005. (© David Portnoy/Getty Images.)

while she met with FEMA. Her reaction was very emotional. She hugged me tightly as she sobbed. Quickly she introduced her children to me and left for the 4th floor. That next hour and a half was one of the longest of my life. The twin girls were as different as night and day. Nakia must have been an ADD child because she was all over the place and all over me, sitting in my lap, lying across my lap, aggravating her sister and hitting herself in the head. Kendra's behavior was the antithesis of Nakia's. She sat quietly playing with donated toys and was very polite and poised. Unfortunately, two-year-old Darren emulated Nakia's behavior instead of Kendra's. I was horrified when Nakia gave him some Play-Dough and he immediately popped it into his mouth. I had to pry his teeth open to get the Play-Dough out. My heart went out to those kids as I tried to keep them occupied. We played "I Spy" and I looked around for a book to read to Darren. A *National Geographic* magazine was the only available reading material, and I read an article to Darren about elephant seals but he preferred to look at the car advertisements so I read the text of the advertisements instead. Volunteers were bringing trays with dinner but Kendra, ever the compliant child, wanted to wait until she had her mother's permission to eat. Over Kendra's objection, I allowed a volunteer to deliver their dinner because it was getting late and they were obviously hungry. Their mother returned with a man she said had offered her a place to stay. I bade them all goodbye and went home exhausted.

The volunteers I've talked to all agree that their efforts helping Katrina victims has been a very rewarding time in their lives. People are grateful not only to be given assistance but to be treated with dignity and respect. If any good could come out of this hurricane, this must be it.

A New Orleans Woman Suffers Post-Traumatic Stress Disorder After Hurricane Katrina

Susannah Breslin

In the following viewpoint, a New Orleans resident relates her experience during Hurricane Katrina. The author was able to evacuate the city before the storm hit, and she watched the aftermath from Lafayette, Louisiana. She recalls her experience once she was able to return to New Orleans and gather her belongings. Six months later, she began experiencing anxiety attacks. It took her years to discover that she developed post-traumatic stress disorder from the storm. This discovery helped her begin the healing process, and she found strength in sharing her story with others. Susannah Breslin is a freelance journalist who has written for *Harper's Bazaar, Details, Newsweek, Salon, Slate,* The Daily Beast, *Marie Claire, Variety, Forbes,* and *Esquire.*

SOURCE. Susannah Breslin, "After Hurricane Katrina, Years of Post-Traumatic Stress," *The Atlantic,* August 29, 2011. Copyright © 2011 Susannah Breslin. All rights reserved. Reproduced with permission.

In 2003, I relocated to New Orleans from California, and two years later, I was living in a neighborhood called the Bywater on a street named for a saint who was flayed alive, six blocks west of the Industrial Canal that would flood the city's Lower 9th Ward. Two blocks from the Mississippi River, I rented half a shotgun—an architectural style popular in New Orleans that gets its nickname from the fact that a person standing at the front door can fire a shotgun directly out the backdoor.

On August 26, 2005, Hurricane Katrina barreled into the Gulf of Mexico. By August 28, it had grown from a Category 3 hurricane to a Category 5 hurricane on the Saffir-Simpson Hurricane Scale with maximum sustained winds within its eyewall clocking in at 175 m.p.h. On the morning of August 29, the cyclone—now a Category 3 with sustained winds of 125 m.p.h.—made landfall near Buras, Louisiana, a small community located at the bottom of the toe of Louisiana's boot-like shape.

From there, the storm swept across St. Bernard Parish, St. Tammany Parish, and east of New Orleans. Continuing north, it slipped over the Louisiana-Mississippi border, and on August 30, it weakened to a tropical depression over the Ten-

> When I did return to New Orleans, the city was ravaged, its great oak trees broken, its buildings crumbling.

nessee Valley. The resultant storm surge produced massive destruction across multiple states, and New Orleans' levees were breached catastrophically, flooding an estimated 80 percent of the Crescent City. The hurricane left 1,836 dead and hundreds missing.

Surviving the Storm

The day before Katrina made landfall, I fled the city, ending up in Lafayette, Louisiana, with a dozen other evacuees. Together, we looked on in paralyzed horror as the city flooded on the TV screen. The Louisiana Superdome became a refugee camp, New Orleans residents waited on rooftops bearing signs asking to be saved, and the dead lay uncollected in the streets. The storm's damage tally would exceed an estimated $80 billion. When it became clear none of us would be going home anytime soon, we left one by one, heading to points across the country.

When I did return to New Orleans, the city was ravaged, its great oak trees broken, its buildings crumbling, a refrigerator stranded on a dark sidewalk like a ghost. My neighborhood was deserted. A sign on the front of the house where I had lived indicated the roof shingles, which had come off during the storm, contained asbestos. I was in the 20 percent of the city that hadn't flooded, but portions of the roof had come off during the storm.

Inside, the rain had spawned black, green, and yellow mold that crawled the walls. I could see the sky from the living room through the exposed wooden slats of the structure's bones. The ceiling was in the bed. In the backyard, a towering pecan tree that had stood for probably 100 years had been uprooted from the ground and tossed aside like a toothpick by a bored giant.

I took the boxes and my papers from the mostly undisturbed kitchen. From the rest of the house, I picked and chose from the things that didn't appear to have mold or asbestos on them. The following day, I drove out of the city. There was a boat in the middle of the street. The houses gaped, slack-jawed and empty-faced. I drove across the eastbound span of the Twin Span Bridge over Lake Pontchartrain, and parts of the westbound span of the bridge were simply gone. I drove an hour through a destroyed forest, and when I looked up in the sky, I tried to imagine a thing so big that it could destroy so much.

The Mental Impact of the Disaster

Six months later, the shock had worn off, and I was numb, dead, like a plug disconnected from a socket. Somewhere along the way, my brain's neural circuitry had been overloaded. A fuse had blown, but I could not find the fuse box. I grew increasingly unable to think well, then to think at all. Broke, I took a job as a waitress, and life became something I witnessed through the wrong end of a kaleidoscope. I was disconnected, enraged, anxious. At night, I would fall asleep, then jerk awake moments later, my arms flailing as if warding off an oncoming attack.

In my dreams, the city was always flooding, even though I had missed the flood. I withdrew from the world. Sometimes I wondered if I was dead, suspended in a kind of posthumous existence in which everything appeared to be real but was a hallucination. It was hard to discern the root cause: Hurricane Katrina, the nervous breakdown I'd had in early 2005, the reporting I did as a journalist in the years prior covering the adult movie industry. Or, perhaps it was some inherent, unseen weakness in a malfunctioning brain that I could not see but that controlled me.

> 'In PTSD the past is relived with an immediate sensory and emotional intensity that makes victims feel as if the event were occurring all over again.'

Over time, I would get better, but it would take several years, and, even then, there would be relapses. On October 13, 2009, four years after the storm made landfall, frustrated by a work-related problem, I walked from the living room of my apartment and into the kitchen. I stopped in front of a cabinet, rocked back on my heels, and slammed my head into the cupboard in front me as hard as I could. Immediately thereafter, I smashed my hand into the neighboring cupboard. In the wake of what had happened, I stood there, reeling.

In a paper called "Posttraumatic Stress Disorder and Memory," Dr. Bessel van der Kolk, a clinical psychiatrist who has studied PTSD [post-traumatic stress disorder] for over three decades, explains how it works. "Ordinarily, memories of particular events are remembered as stories that change and deteriorate over time and that do not evoke intense emotions and sensations," van der Kolk writes. "In contrast, in PTSD the past is relived with an immediate sensory and emotional intensity that makes victims feel as if the event were occurring all over again." Simply put, one experiences a traumatic event but is unable to integrate it into the story of his or her life.

Why did I develop PTSD while some whose lives were more greatly devastated by Hurricane Katrina did not?

According to van der Kolk, it depends on whether or not one dissociates from the traumatic event. If the event is never fully experienced, it fails to be integrated into a "past-tense" narrative, leaving the survivor living in the shadow of a memory-in-limbo—an experience playing over and over again on an internal JumboTron with no remote control. As a result, some disconnect emotionally; others fail to remember at all. "For example, traumatized people may know what has happened to them, but they may have no feelings about it," van der Kolk adds. "Conversely, people may act disturbed without knowing what makes them behave that way."

Explaining PTSD

This past July [2011], I was asked to appear on National Public Radio's "Talk of the Nation" to discuss the White House's decision to send condolence letters to families of servicemen and servicewomen who commit suicide while deployed in combat zones.

During the program, the conversation turned to post-traumatic stress disorder and some of its symptoms: hyper-vigilance, flashbacks, emotional numbness, night terrors, anger, depression, anxiety, and an exaggerated fight-or-flight response. The host, Neal Conan, asked me about my personal experience with PTSD, and I attempted to explain what it was like. I said that it was like looking at life through a pane of smoked glass. I told him that you become "emotionally dead."

After the show aired, I received an email from Brad Fleegle, 27, a Marine corporal and Iraq War veteran who lives in Portland, Oregon.

"I've often told people that I feel like there's a glass barrier between myself and everyone else," his email read, in part. "I can see them, but I can't connect and communicate with them. I am alone in a small glass box, seemingly within the world but actually removed from it."

Not every combat veteran emerges from war with this sense of dislocation. For some, an extreme life experience—war, trauma, a natural disaster—can give their lives new meaning. After the hurricane, I relocated to Virginia, where, working on a story for the local newspaper, I interviewed J.R. Martinez, a then-22-year-old Army corporal from Shreveport, Louisiana. Martinez had suffered burns over 40 percent of his body when he drove a Humvee over a landmine in Karbala, Iraq, and was trapped inside.

> Those who witness stories bigger than themselves have a responsibility to tell their stories and keep telling them.

At a fundraiser where he was helping raise money for other veterans injured in Iraq and Afghanistan, Martinez pulled off his knit cap to show me the breast implant that was embedded under the skin of his skull to expand the skin, which would be grafted onto other, scarred parts of his body. I suggested that when he was done with it, he donate the breast implant to a stripper who had only one breast implant, and we laughed. At the time, Martinez had undergone over two-dozen surgeries. For the most part, he was cheery and upbeat. It seemed through what had happened to him, he had found his purpose.

In 2010, I started interviewing combat veterans and launched The War Project. Some of the veterans I meet are struggling with their experiences; others are not.

They have been to Iraq, Afghanistan, and sometimes both. On one end of the spectrum is Hart Viges, an Army mortarman-turned-conscientious objector who had a religious revelation during a post-deployment screening of "The Passion of the Christ" and now dresses up like Jesus, walking around town holding a sign that reads "JESUS AGAINST WAR." On the other is George Zubaty, who deployed to Afghanistan in 2002 and Iraq in 2003 and has the cool unflappability of a politician-to-be. Zubaty told me, "All the times when I shot at somebody in Iraq, it never really struck me as being something that I was gonna internalize as some kind of, like, great metaphysical wrong."

It's been six years since Hurricane Katrina made landfall and two years since I slammed my head into a cupboard on purpose. Over the years, I've come to understand those who witness stories bigger than themselves have a responsibility to tell their stories and keep telling them. It's through this process that we come to terms with what happened, and, in doing so, we are able to move on, even as we look at the past. It's a way to keep from dissociating, to weave our memories more firmly into the stories of our lives.

A Katrina Survivor Explains the Lifelong Process of Recovery

Allison Good

In the following viewpoint, a Hurricane Katrina survivor reflects on the storm's impact five years after it made landfall. Life after the storm was a complex process, the author explains—one that made her life richer, but also involved a traumatic emotional recovery. After the storm, she fell in love with New Orleans, and she has been inspired by the positive changes that have occurred in the city. However, the author writes, she will never forget the death and destruction caused by the hurricane. On the storm's fifth anniversary, the author comes to the realization that recovering from the storm cannot be measured in months or years—instead it will be a lifelong process. At the time of this viewpoint, Allison Good was a freelance writer and political science student at Vassar College in Poughkeepsie, New York.

If you could wave a magic wand, go back to mid-August 2005, and live your life from there, would you do it?

A friend asked me this question a few weeks ago as we discussed the upcoming fifth anniversary of Hurricane Katrina [August 2010], which devastated our city and our psyches. I answered that if I could relocate my pre-Katrina house to an area that did not flood when the underfunded and poorly constructed 17th Street Canal broke, I would not wave that magic wand. Oh no, he replied, it's a yes or no answer, no ifs, ands, or buts allowed. All or nothing. After experiencing the initial shock of losing my house and my two cats, the four months spent in limbo in a rental house in Atlanta, and a long and harrowing emotional recovery, I was surprised to hear myself say, absolutely not, I would never want to go back in time and live as if Katrina had never happened.

Falling in Love with New Orleans

This unusual query caught me off-guard. I had never been asked this before, and most people with a conservative sense of decorum would probably think it inappropriate and impolite to even wonder. It's not a popular hypothetical, not around here where people are still unable to rebuild their homes and overcome post-traumatic stress disorder, but my life is much richer because of Katrina. I have fallen in love with New Orleans. When I was a sophomore in high school, I couldn't wait to relocate to the northeast. In July 2005 I was living a sheltered life in a suburban-esque community on the outskirts of the city, but these days I enjoy hanging out in my center hall cottage in Faubourg-St. John, just three blocks from the bayou. I listen to [New Orleans singers] Irma Thomas and Dr. John, look for Mardi Gras

> There's no doubt that the city is coming back, and New Orleans has become a dynamic experiment in grassroots organizing.

Indians on Super Sunday, and dissect the minutiae of each episode of [the HBO series] *Treme*. Five years ago, I was oblivious when it came to such cultural gems.

My perceptions about positive change, however, are not limited to myself. There's no doubt that the city is coming back, and New Orleans has become a dynamic experiment in grassroots organizing. People from all over the world have relocated here because they want to help out. Liz McCartney's St. Bernard Project has been so successful that it is no longer rebuilding those houses destroyed in St. Bernard during Katrina, but beginning construction on new homes. Hundreds of college graduates have participated in Teach for America, doing their part to repair and reform our broken school system. Young entrepreneurs are moving here in droves to be a part of a great renaissance. Something special is happening here.

And then I watched Sunday's *Dateline NBC*, Brian Williams' self-described time capsule of the first five days after the storm and his reflections on the devastation and helplessness, and realized I must retract my answer. It was my first time seeing a lot of those images and videos that became so famous, because during those five days my parents did their best to shield all of us from the twenty-four-hour news networks. Since then I have seen photographs of my own flooded-out home and neighborhood, read Anderson Cooper's memoir about reporting from disaster sites, and stay up to date on the Danziger Bridge police shootings.

Surviving the Death and Destruction

It took me a few years to be able to talk about any of it, more years to feel like I could read about it and now, for the first time, I'm writing about it. My family has stayed strong, I suffered nothing more than extreme grief and mild depression, and I thought I was doing pretty well. But how do you react to emaciated bodies in wheelchairs, dead from dehydration, starvation, and lack of emergency medical care? You cry to the point of physical exhaustion. I bawled when Williams started to talk about all of the pets swimming in that toxic water or wandering the empty streets, because all I could think about were my two cats that drowned in the six feet of water that the 17th Street Canal unleashed on our neighborhood.

> The bad can never outweigh the five years of progress, but Katrina happened. . . . And I'll be recovering for the rest of my life.

As a student of political science, I am quite familiar with [philosopher] Thomas Hobbes' anarchic state of nature and his famous observation that life is nasty, brutish, and short. It was, however, only a theory. No one had ever witnessed such an environment, but then Katrina happened. Williams made sure to include a lot of footage that showed homeless refugees looting the stores on Canal Street in broad daylight, stealing eight boxes of Nike sneakers at a time or scrounging for diapers and toilet paper, while others fired at policemen. Now I know that Hobbes wasn't kidding, and what I saw Sunday night was both shocking and paralyzing. It dealt a devastating blow to whatever iota of confidence had prompted me to say that my post-Katrina life was better, unthinkable after that hour-long reminder of all the death and destruction.

At this point, I don't have an answer to that question. The bad can never outweigh the five years of progress, but Katrina happened. As author Louis Maistros wrote in an August issue of the [New Orleans] *Times-Picayune*, "What happened to us in the summer of 2005 isn't something you recover from. It's something that you stand up to if you're able, and it's something you may conspire to defy if you choose—but you never really recover from it." Truer words were never said. I had considered myself to be recovered, but on this five-year anniversary I have to face reality: My name is Allison Good, and I'll be recovering for the rest of my life.

CHRONOLOGY

August 23, 2005   The National Hurricane Center in Miami issues an advisory that the season's twelfth tropical depression has formed over the Bahamas. (The 2005 Atlantic hurricane season was the most active season in recorded history; twenty-eight tropical and subtropical storms formed, and fifteen became hurricanes.)

August 24   The tropical storm strengthens and is named Katrina. Florida governor Jeb Bush declares a state of emergency in southern Florida.

August 25   Katrina is now a category-one hurricane. The eye of the storm hits Florida's southeastern coast with winds up to 80 miles per hour.

August 26   The storm's center emerges from the Florida peninsula and strengthens in the Gulf of Mexico. Louisiana governor Kathleen Blanco and Mississippi governor Haley Barbour declare states of emergency.

August 28   Hurricane Katrina becomes a category-five storm, and the National Hurricane Center predicts it will overtop levees in New Orleans.

New Orleans mayor Ray Nagin issues a mandatory evacuation order, and tens of thousands of residents leave the city. Many residents who are unable to leave town seek shelter in the Louisiana Superdome.

August 29   Hurricane Katrina, having weakened to a category-three storm, hits the Gulf Coast, causing damage in

Louisiana, Mississippi, and Alabama; President George W. Bush declares Louisiana and Mississippi major disaster areas.

A major levee in New Orleans fails, and the city begins to flood.

August 30 Floodwaters continue to pour into New Orleans from breaks in the city's levees, and 80 percent of the low-lying city is underwater. Governor Blanco orders that all remaining residents leave New Orleans—including those staying in the Superdome.

August 31 Secretary of the US Department of Health and Human Services Michael O. Leavitt declares a public health emergency in Louisiana, Mississippi, Alabama, and Florida.

Reports of criminal activity in New Orleans move the military to increase National Guard deployment in the area, and a curfew is imposed on the city.

September 1 Mayor Nagin pleads for help from the federal government; he claims there is no food for residents in the Superdome and the New Orleans Convention Center.

Buses and helicopters begin to take evacuees from the Superdome stadium to Baton Rouge, Louisiana, and Houston, Texas.

September 2 US Congress approves $10.5 billion in aid for rescue and relief in the aftermath of Hurricane Katrina; National Guard troops distribute food and water to New Orleans residents in the Superdome and convention center; and President Bush tours areas affected by Hurricane Katrina and commends the performance of Federal Emergency Management Agency (FEMA) director Michael Brown.

September 3	A huge airlift operation rescues thousands of survivors from New Orleans, and more than ten thousand people are removed from the area.
September 4	The United States asks for international aid from the North Atlantic Treaty Organization (NATO) and the European Union in the aftermath of Hurricane Katrina.
September 5	Some New Orleans residents are allowed to return to the area to inspect the damage to their homes; engineers continue to work on repairing levee breaks.
September 6	Engineers repair a key breach in New Orleans' floodwalls and begin pumping water from the city. Facing criticism from the US public about the government's response to Hurricane Katrina, President Bush says he will lead an investigation into how the disaster was handled.
September 7	Health concerns arise in New Orleans as floodwater is found to hold dangerous levels of bacteria and lead.
September 8	President Bush declares Friday, September 16, a national day of remembrance for those who lost their lives in the aftermath of Hurricane Katrina; Congress approves an additional $52 billion for the Hurricane Katrina relief effort.
September 9	Brown is removed from his role of managing the Hurricane Katrina relief effort for FEMA; he is replaced by Coast Guard Vice Admiral Thad W. Allen. The US public pledges around $587 million in aid for Hurricane Katrina relief.
September 12	Brown resigns as director of FEMA.

September 23–24   Hurricane Rita makes landfall just west of the Gulf Coast area hardest hit by Hurricane Katrina. New rainfall and strong winds worsen the crisis in the area.

October 14   The official death toll from Hurricane Katrina stands at 1,836 with more than 2,500 still missing.

FOR FURTHER READING

Books

Robert Block and Christopher Cooper, *Disaster: Hurricane Katrina and the Failure of Homeland Security*. New York: Times Books, 2006.

Douglas Brinkley, *The Great Deluge: Hurricane Katrina, New Orleans and the Mississippi Gulf Coast*. New York: HarperCollins, 2006.

Denise Danna and Sandra Cordray, *Nursing in the Storm: Voices from Hurricane Katrina*. New York: Springer, 2009.

Sheri Fink, *Five Days at Memorial: Life and Death in a Storm-Ravaged Hospital*. New York: Crown, 2013.

Jed Horne, *Breach of Faith: Hurricane Katrina and the Near Death of a Great American City*. New York: Random House, 2006.

Phyllis Montana-Leblanc, *Not Just the Levees Broke: My Story During and After Hurricane Katrina*. New York: Atria Books, 2008.

James Patterson Smith, *Hurricane Katrina: The Mississippi Story*. Jackson, MS: University Press of Mississippi, 2012.

Gregory Squires and Chester Hartman, eds., *There is No Such Thing as a Natural Disaster: Race, Class, and Hurricane Katrina*. New York: Routledge, 2006.

Ivor van Heerden and Mike Bryan, *The Storm: What Went Wrong and Why During Hurricane Katrina—The Inside Story from One Louisiana Scientist*. New York: Viking Penguin, 2006.

Lola Vollen and Chris Ying, eds., *Voices from the Storm: The People of New Orleans on Hurricane Katrina and Its Aftermath*. San Francisco: McSweeney's, 2006.

Periodicals

Raymond J. Burby, "Hurricane Katrina and the Paradoxes of Government Disaster Policy: Bringing About Wise Governmental Decisions for Hazardous Areas," *ANNALS of the American Academy of Political and Social Science*, March 2006, vol. 604, no. 1, pp. 171–191.

Neil deMause, "Katrina's Vanishing Victims: Media Forget the 'Rediscovered' Poor," FAIR, August 1, 2006. http://fair.org.

Jason Deparle, "The Nation: Cast Away; Broken Levees, Unbroken Barriers," *New York Times*, September 4, 2005. www.ny times.com.

"Eight Years After Hurricane Katrina, Many Evacuees Yet to Return," *Al Jazeera*, August 29, 2013. http://america.aljazeera .com.

Peter Grier, "The Great Katrina Migration," *Christian Science Monitor*, September 12, 2005. www.csmonitor.com.

"Hurricane Katrina: The Shaming of America," *The Economist*, September 8, 2005. www.economist.com.

Ylan Q. Mui, "Five Years After Katrina, New Orleans Sees Higher Percentage of Hispanics," *Washington Post*, August 21, 2010. www.washingtonpost.com.

David G. Ortiz and Stephen F. Ostertag, "Katrina Bloggers and the Development of Collective Civic Action: The Web as a Virtual Mobilizing Structure," *Sociological Perspectives*, March 2014, vol. 57, no. 1, pp. 52–78.

Jean Rhodes et al., "The Impact of Hurricane Katrina on the Mental and Physical Health of Low-Income Parents in New Orleans," *American Journal of Orthopsychiatry*, vol. 80, April 2010, pp. 237–247.

Saundra K. Schneider, "Administrative Breakdowns in the Governmental Response to Hurricane Katrina," *Public Administration Review*, September/October 2005, vol. 65, no. 5.

Samuel R. Sommers, Evan P. Apfelbaum, Kristin N. Dukes, Negin Toosi, and Elsie J. Wang, "Race and Media Coverage of Hurricane Katrina: Analysis, Implications, and Future Research Questions," *Analyses of Social Issues and Public Policy*, 2006, vol. 6, no. 1, pp. 1–17.

Stacy Teicher, "New Orleans Goes All In on Charter Schools. Is It Showing the Way?," *Christian Science Monitor*, March 1, 2014. www.csmonitor.com.

Kathleen Tierney, "Metaphors Matter: Disaster Myths, Media Frames, and Their Consequences in Hurricane Katrina," *ANNALS of the American Academy of Political and Social Science*, March 2006, vol. 604, no. 1, pp. 57–81.

Websites

The Data Center (www.datacenterresearch.org). The Data Center is a resource for data about southeast Louisiana that focuses on disaster recovery, regional economic analysis, workforce development, racial disparity indicators, and population movements. Also available on the website is the organization's *New Orleans Index*, a biennial publication that was developed after Hurricane Katrina and tracks economic growth, sustainability, and quality of life in the region.

Hurricane Digital Memory Bank (http://hurricanearchive .org). The *Hurricane Digital Memory Bank* is a website that collects and preserves the stories and digital record of Hurricanes Katrina and Rita.

Hurricane Katrina (http://hurricanekatrina.web.unc.edu/eco nomic-suffrage-after-katrina). Maintained by students at the University of North Carolina at Chapel Hill, this website is devoted to tracking the devastating impacts of Hurricane Katrina on public health, politics, and the economy.

Hurricane Katrina: Nine Years After Hurricane Katrina, A Look at Then and Now (www.nola.com/katrina). On this site, the *Times-Picayune* offers an archive of its coverage of Hurricane Katrina, forums for survivors to share their stories, and reflective articles nine years after the storm.

Hurricanes Katrina and Rita: The School Impact (www.ed week.org/ew/collections/hurricane-katrina). This website offers a series of articles focusing on the impact of Hurricanes Katrina and Rita on the public school systems in New Orleans, Alabama, and Mississippi.

INDEX